Before Belief

Emerging Perspectives in Pastoral Theology and Care

Series Editor: Kirk Bingaman, Fordham University

The field of pastoral care and counseling, and by extension pastoral theology, is presently at a crossroads, in urgent need of redefining itself for the age of postmodernity or even post-postmodernity. While there is, to be sure, a rich historical foundation upon which the field can build, it remains for contemporary scholars, educators, and practitioners to chart new directions for the present day and age. Emerging Perspectives in Pastoral Theology and Care seeks to meet this pressing need by inviting researchers in the field to address timely issues, such as the findings of contemplative neuroscience, the impact of technology on human development and wellness, mindfulness meditation practice for reducing anxiety, trauma viewed through the lens of positive psychology and resilience theory, clergy health and wellness, postmodern and multicultural pastoral care and counseling, and issues of race and class. The series will therefore serve as an important and foundational resource for years to come, guiding scholars and educators in the field in developing more contemporary models of theory and practice.

Titles in the Series

Before Belief: Discovering First Spiritual Awareness, by Bruce A. Stevens
Warriors between Worlds: Moral Injury and Identities in Crisis, by Zachary Moon
Pastoral and Spiritual Care in a Digital Age: The Future Is Now, by Kirk Bingaman
Women Leaving Prison: Justice-Seeking Spiritual Support for Female Returning Citizens,
    by Jill L. Snodgrass
The Chaplain's Presence and Medical Power: Rethinking Loss in the Hospital System,
    by Richard Coble
Neuroplasticity, Performativity, and Clergy Wellness: Neighbor Love as Self-Care,
    by William D. Roozeboom

Before Belief

Discovering First Spiritual Awareness

Bruce A. Stevens

LEXINGTON BOOKS
Lanham • Boulder • New York • London

Published by Rowman & Littlefield
Lexington Books is an imprint of The Rowman & Littlefield Publishing Group, Inc.
4501 Forbes Boulevard, Suite 200, Lanham, Maryland 20706
www.rowman.com

6 Tinworth Street, London SE11 5AL, United Kingdom

British Library Cataloguing in Publication Information Available

Library of Congress Cataloging-in-Publication Data Available

ISBN 9781793607218 (cloth : alk. paper)
ISBN 9781793607225 (electronic)

Dedicated to my grandchildren:
Jade, Levi, Ayla, Zachary, Emmett, Orlando, and Audrey.
I am grateful.

Contents

Introduction   1

1   Some Maps   7

2   First Things First   17

3   From One Generation to the Next   23

4   The Senses   33

5   Sight   45

6   Touch (including the Sense of Body)   51

7   Hearing   61

8   Smell   65

9   Taste   69

10 Revisiting Infantile Experience   75

11 Into Language   83

12 Evaluation   93

13 Now for Integration   103

14 Committed Living   111

15 Early Spirituality in Ministry   119

Conclusion   129

Appendix: The Early Spirituality Profile   131

Bibliography   133

Index   143

About the Author   147

Introduction

First things are spiritually important. Awareness comes with the first breath—or possibly before, at conception or in the womb.[1] This leads to significant questions: How do early experiences make us who we are? What is an infant's first sense of mystery or transcendence? When might God make an entrance? At present, we have more questions than answers, but that may soon change. Developmental researchers have made many advances that can fundamentally change how we see spiritual formation.

This book explores our earliest spiritual awareness in infancy, before language and cognitive understanding. Research has established that babies learn from birth. This indicates what might be called a reservoir of proto-learning, which is *before belief* because ideas come much later.[2] There is no exact word for what is being described, so I will use "unconscious spiritual learning," which I hope will function as a signpost pointing to what is formative of the spiritual self.

While all this is unconscious, the best description is not Freud's notion of the unconscious or Jung's collective unconscious, including archetypes. This book identifies a nonconscious learning process. Various terms have been used, such as "implicit learning" and "tacit knowledge," which are discussed in the first chapter. For the moment, I propose using a developmental lens to see personal growth encompassing the physical, emotional, psychological, and, of course, spiritual realms.[3]

The implications are many. I invite you to explore some exciting ideas about the origins of our spirituality. As the author of this book, I have the modest role of a tourist guide, simply indicating the sights. But the points of interest will seem exotic because this territory has been largely unexplored. This learning model, which goes back to infant awareness, is unique in the pastoral care literature.

WHO SHOULD READ THIS BOOK?

Clergy, chaplains, spiritual directors, pastoral counselors, and mental health professionals are likely to be interested in early spiritual formation. These spiritual leaders will appreciate what has been missing in the discussion up to now.

I will point out some of the unfortunate consequences of ignoring unconscious spiritual learning. For example, we can end up doing ministry blind. It is like the children's game of pin the tail on the donkey. We begin with generalized assumptions about the person we are seeking to help (after all, the donkey is there somewhere), but easily miss the distinctives of what needs to change. Almost always there are elements of dysfunctional learning. That learning, once discovered, can be very specific. The blindfold is taken off!

The model of unconscious spiritual learning opens new understanding of some common difficulties in ministry. For example, church people can be rigid and dogmatic. When something is learned at an early age, *it feels true*. It does not matter whether the belief is right or wrong; it will carry a sense of certainty. This also explains why some beliefs are irrational. Since unconscious learning begins early in cognitive development, it happens before there is any capacity for evaluation, so it is taken in as if through a vacuum cleaner, and everything is accepted. This is understandable if the source is parents or authority figures, but it can result in ill-informed assumptions about "the way things are." And, if what has been learned remains inarticulate, there is no possibility of developing a counter-narrative, so that early learning will go unchallenged and remain a silent influence.

We tend to act in ways consistent with early learning:

> *Marg* had recently joined a Reformed church.[4] She was talking to her pastor and was having some difficulty understanding what seemed an important message: "I don't understand it when you talk about God's grace. Doesn't God set the standards for how we're expected to behave as Christians?" Marg grew up in a strict, somewhat legalistic, home. In this case, her early learning proved to be a barrier to her understanding the unconditional love of God.

The process of learning is probably the same regardless of content. Everything is just learned: that is the way the brain operates. Experiences are brought together, and learning is in the connection. This includes early relational understanding, with implications for psychological development, and it appears to be the same process leading to spiritual development. Normally, there is both positive and negative input, resulting in both adaptive and dysfunctional patterns of behavior, although the balance may differ from person to person and family to family.

These examples are simply to whet your appetite for exploring further implications of early learning. It is at first an unconscious process. Initial input comes prior to cognitive development or any possibility of questioning the content. This is true for both early emotional and early spiritual development.

Reflect: The insight about early learning brings a new focus to pastoral care. We can consider what the person learned in early childhood and beyond.

FURTHER EXAMPLES

We can see that early learning is a major factor in determining personality, but it is usually a mixed bag. The focus is largely on the meeting (or not) of infantile needs, with positive or negative results. A sad case of early learning is the baby who learns *not* to cry. If early needs are neglected, there is no point in crying because it will go unheeded. Ironically, the unobservant parent will often say something like, "She's such a good baby. She never cries."

Early learning has echoes in pastoral and clinical experience. Compare the following cases:

> *Sally* had a hard life. Her mother was addicted to heroin. She never knew her father, who left before Sally was born. She was subjected to a merry-go-round of adult male figures who came in and out of her life. A number were violent and abusive. The only constants in her life were neglect, uncertainty, and a lack of safety. After her mother died of an overdose, Sally had a dramatic conversion experience and began to attend a Pentecostal church.

> *Nick* was raised in a "white picket fence" family. There was never a lot of money, since his father was the pastor of a small rural United Church congregation. His mother had social work qualifications but chose the role of a stay-at-home mother. Nick knew he was loved. He always had a sense of God: "There was never a time I didn't believe, although my faith was challenged when I was at university. But I always came back 'home' in more of a sense than just visiting my parents!"

Sally and Nick had very different early childhood experiences. A psychologist would predict that Sally might be more psychologically vulnerable than Nick. She had experiences that often led to chronic psychological disturbance, or what a clinician might diagnose as a personality disorder. Difficulties are "woven into the fabric" of who she is. Becoming a Christian does not magically remove her psychological vulnerability. Additionally, that hothouse of early life experiences may result in different spiritual attitudes. For example, it would be hardly surprising if Sally experiences God as unreliable and even capricious, whereas Nick has a more comfortable and secure relationship with God.[5]

Early experiences of nurture can be observed to be either mostly good or mostly bad, but they are always mixed. Both negative and positive life experiences shape us in profound ways—especially when we are young and most vulnerable. It is not surprising that we all have a mixed bag of psychological and spiritual, positive and negative, true and false learning. Sally and Nick illustrate this well.

What is the way forward? The focus of this book is on unconscious spiritual learning. We will see that such beliefs are largely unconscious, but expressed in various ways; hidden but discoverable; and inarticulate, but can be put into words.

SUMMARY

The reformer John Calvin said, "Our wisdom . . . consists almost entirely of two parts: knowledge of God and of ourselves."[6] The premise of this book is that both matter.

How do we understand the origins of spiritual development? The argument here is that we need to go back to our earliest learning, which occurs before we gain the ability to speak and think abstractly. Those experiences are formative not only of our personality but also of our developing spirituality and our understanding of God. This is, of course, a bold claim, but what comes in the following pages will support this thesis and outline various ways to apply what we discover.

This book is part of a series on pastoral care. There is a practical dimension both in the book and in practice modules on the www.earlyspirituality .com website. Those exercises can be used in ministry or spiritual direction. Treat the suggestions as a smorgasbord—use what interests you and ignore the rest. Photocopy any exercises you think might be helpful for study groups or to those you are helping in ministry. Everything will initially be somewhat fuzzy as we begin our exploration, but I hope what is spiritually significant will come into sharper focus. This book has been written with ministers in mind, but the theme of hidden spiritual learning may interest a lay readership as well, or indeed anyone hoping to understand more about their spiritual development. These ideas are too important to be left to the professionals!

NOTES

1. See research by Lei Cao-Lei, Guillaume Elgbeili, Renaud Massart, David P. Laplante, Moshe Szyf, and Suzanne King, "Pregnant women's cognitive appraisal of

a natural disaster affects DNA methylation in their children 13 years later: Project Ice Storm," *Translational Psychiatry*, 2015, 5:e515, doi:10.1038/tp.2015.13.

2. For a review, although most of the focus is on later development, see Chris J. Boyatzis, "Spiritual development during childhood and adolescence," in Lisa J. Miller (ed.), *The Oxford Handbook of Psychology and Spirituality*, Oxford University Press, New York, 2012, 151–64.

3. I have extensively cited academic and other sources. As an academic, I want to avoid any possibility of plagiarism, and the references allow the reader to follow up topics of interest.

4. Marg, like others cited in this book, is illustrative and drawn from my pastoral and therapeutic experience. She does not correspond to a specific person. Nor does anyone in the study group or extended case studies.

5. See attachment patterns in Virginia L. Colin, *Human attachment*, McGraw-Hill, New Jersey, 1996.

6. Book 1, Chapter 1, Part 1, John Calvin, *Calvin's institutes of the Christian religion*, MacDonald Publishing Co., MacDill, Florida, no date, 7.

Chapter One

Some Maps

You stub your toe. Ouch! This is the easiest way to learn that something is hard. Essentially, learning is the meaningful connection of different experiences. Rock and pain. But nothing can ever be left that simple. Distinctions are made between classical conditioning, operant conditioning, and social learning that are best explained in countless psychology textbooks. Here, the focus is very specific: early or unconscious learning and its spiritual implications.

There have been a number of attempts to chart the wordless realm of early learning. All have some validity, but most of the researchers make no attempt to grasp mystery, transcendence, or an experience of God. And yet, all potentially contribute to our understanding of early spiritual influences. There is a technical focus in this chapter, which reviews research from a number of disciplines, and this will provide a foundation for what follows.

CONCEPTUAL PERSPECTIVES

Sigmund Freud, in developing psychoanalytic theory, explored the unconscious.[1] He saw a range of mental activities occurring automatically and not readily available to conscious reflection. This includes memories, motivations, repressed feelings, desires, instincts, automatic skills, subliminal perceptions, habits, and automatic reactions.[2]

Carl Jung broke from an early allegiance to Freud to establish a different approach to the unconscious. He saw it as containing a store of repressed memories for the individual. In the unconscious there is an interaction of systems, including ego, complexes, and archetypes.[3] He also proposed a collective unconscious including archetypes. Although Jung's theories were often speculative, he has the advantage of being more sympathetic to a religious worldview than Freud. There have been books exploring similarities and applying his insights to pastoral care.[4]

More recently, John Kihlstrom drew on cognitive science for his understanding of the cognitive unconscious. In the journal *Science*, he noted that "a great deal of information processing takes place outside of working memory."[5] He reviewed research in areas such as automatic processes, subliminal perception, implicit memory, and hypnotic alterations to underline the importance of this in cognitive science generally. Kihlstrom's approach was also broad, and he concluded that the unconscious was important: "There are, within the domain of procedural knowledge, a number of complex processes that are inaccessible to introspection."[6] It is important to make connections because without them certain aspects of mental life are dissociated from awareness and are not accompanied by the experience of consciousness.[7]

Note that all these approaches to the unconscious involve something of a grab bag of unconscious processes that are more extensive than learning something without words. The idea of a learning process that begins before there is a capacity for words brings clarity to these murky waters. I hope we will see its application to pastoral care.

There is considerable precedent for a focus on learning, as is evident from diverse research studies. It is evident in what Michael Polanyi described as "tacit knowledge," which results in a knowing beyond words to express: "This ineffable domain of skillful knowing is continuous in its inarticulateness with the knowledge possessed by animals and infants, who . . . also possess the capacity for re-organizing their inarticulate knowledge and using it as an interpretive framework."[8] Later, Polanyi noted that we know more than we can tell.[9] Tacit knowledge is the result of what Arthur Reber called "implicit learning." He introduced that term in his 1965 master's thesis, and he developed an understanding of the concept through a lifetime of research. He offered this definition: "[I]mplicit learning is the acquisition of knowledge that takes place largely independently of conscious attempts to learn and largely in the absence of explicit knowledge about what was acquired."[10] Both the tacit knowledge and implicit learning theses are limited in not acknowledging that such learning can be dysfunctional. I will return to implicit learning in a later chapter.

The French scholar Pierre Bourdieu provided a more social perspective.[11] Power is culturally created and constantly relegitimized through an interplay of agency and structure. He developed the idea of *habitus*, which was his term for socialized norms or tendencies that guide behavior and thinking, which includes tastes, predispositions, and unconscious thought patterns.

Bruce Ecker referred to "emotional learning" in his coherence therapy.[12] Unfortunately, the term is somewhat misleading. There is too much emphasis placed on the emotional dimension when the mechanism includes unconscious cognitive processes (which may or may not have an emotional quality). Coherence therapy has developed a number of useful ways to discover this learning, which can be applied more widely. It has also been adapted to include a Christian approach to psychotherapy, but the approach is conservative and not very nuanced.[13] Other therapies, such as cognitive behavioral therapy, acknowledge a nonconscious dimension as well.[14]

The neurosciences provide another perspective. The newborn's brain has been described as "plastic,"[15] but the parts differ in flexibility. Paul McLean distinguished the reptilian, mammalian, and human parts of the brain.[16] The brain stem (which we have in common with reptiles) is the least complex and most resistant to change, while the "higher" frontal cortex (which is highly developed in humans) is the most complex and highly adaptive. This is useful and has implications for how different parts of the brain learn—for example, processes in the "lower" parts are mostly unconscious.

Reflect: Think about some of the activities that you do but find it hard to describe how. You may know how to ride a push-bike or how to use a bow to shoot an arrow. You can probably recognize the face of Pope Francis. Presumably, you know how to act appropriately in a social situation. You might have a sense of when it feels safe to share something about yourself with a new acquaintance, or know how to cope emotionally after a change in your life. And this just touches the surface of the countless important things we have learned but lack words to describe.

All the writers whom I have mentioned acknowledge that there is an important "knowing" that happens outside conscious awareness. It is present at birth. This learning is associated with the emotions, resides in the body, is expressed in automatic skills, and can remain inarticulate. More conscious learning is cognitive, comes with language, focuses on facts, and begins to be evident in three-year-olds.[17] Christopher Bollas, a Freudian analyst, used the term "unthought knowns,"[18] which is a useful label, but his understanding was restricted by psychoanalytic assumptions.

This review of theoretical approaches is not exhaustive, but indicates areas of relevant research. Note that, with rare exceptions, such understanding has not shed any light on spiritual development. However, the "attachment" paradigm is different. Here, extensive research has been applied to a believer's relationship with God.

ATTACHMENT THEORY AND GOD

Attachment theory developed from the work of John Bowlby, another psychoanalyst. This theory offers four patterns of attachment between children and their parents or carers.[19] The patterns are determined early In the first year and are clearly evident by eighteen months. If a child's needs are met, the infant's assumption is that people are dependable. If not, attachment becomes anxious in different ways.

The research into attachment patterns involved watching how young children behave using the "strange situation" test.[20] It was found that toddlers relate to adults in a variety of ways. The following patterns have been identified:

- *A style is avoidant.* This child is comfortable being alone. She uses her resources to meet her personal needs. Her basic assumption might be: "Better to rely on yourself than to trust anyone."
- *B style is healthy.* The child has enough relational stability to either depend on others or be autonomous. The adult is used as a "safe base" to explore the environment.
- *C style is ambivalent.* He has a strong need to attach to others but has little confidence in emotional self-regulation. His core belief could be: "You have to take care that people like you, but you can never fully trust them!"
- *D style is mixed (disorganized).* This is a confused style of attachment with little internal consistency. It is often present in survivors of childhood trauma and those who have suffered severe neglect. Her mood and behavior may shift in unpredictable ways.

The attachment paradigm is a theory of early unconscious learning. It has influenced a range of disciplines. Attachment patterns are considered to be foundational to later relationships: someone anxiously attached as a two-year-old is likely to have anxious relationships at age thirty or later. Patricia Crittendon extended the attachment model to include adult categories of attachment,[21] but the origins are early, as we have seen. The patterns are learned before language and hence are an expression of unconscious learning.

It is equally possible to think of a believer's relationship to God in terms of attachment styles.[22]

- *A style is avoidant.* Christians are commonly avoidant in relating to God: "Let me get on with my life." Of course, some will attend worship but not expect to relate to God.
- *B style is healthy.* There is enough relational stability to connect with God and to use personal resources in a flexible way. This healthy attachment can take many forms, but each will be characterized by the confidence that "I know God will be there for me if things go wrong."
- *C style is ambivalent.* This kind of attachment is spiritually unstable. The person may have periods of great enthusiasm for the faith, but that does

not last. Perhaps his commitment to a church is erratic, perhaps leading to disappointment followed by lasting bitterness. He may say something like, "God is really important, but isn't really there for me when I most need help."

• *D style is mixed (disorganized).* This confused style of attachment plays out in the spiritual realm as well. She shows no consistency in relating to God, attending church or carrying out a ministry. Her inner spiritual world is chaotic.

This early learning is translated through attachment "filters." It is like a hidden code that links early learning with later behavior.[23] Indeed, attachment theory provides a perspective on what an individual might expect in the interpersonal realm, with implications for their relationship with God. This is explored in the popular book *God Attachment* by Tim Clinton and Joshua Straub.[24]

Attachment theory is a huge advance and is supported by an impressive body of research. Its implications for spiritual development have been explored, with interesting results, but it is essentially relational and typically dyadic in focus. It is just one slice of the pie, as we will see. Early learning touches many areas.

SELF-ESTEEM: A PRACTICAL ILLUSTRATION

The concept of unconscious spiritual learning is broad. There are many applications. I will illustrate this with a brief look at low self-esteem.[25]

Not everyone values themselves. You can think about this on a spectrum from underappreciating personal strengths to a profound self-loathing. Why does this occur? I think of Princess Diana, the celebrity princess of my generation. Apparently, she had it all: fame, beauty, wealth, aristocratic blue blood, and loyal friends. She was human, of course, and had difficulties in her marriage to a king-in-waiting. However, if the tabloids are to be believed, she was not happy. She may have been admired but she was plagued by chronic low self-esteem. If we think about such an attitude to the self, it cannot be rational, since one does not *earn* one's value as a person. The biblical perspective is that we are created as the *imago dei* and are highly valued (Genesis 1.26). Our value is given by the Creator, who does not make "junk."

Low self-esteem is a *felt sense* of having no value. Initially, it is a belief without propositions. It is another example of unconscious learning, perhaps gained in the first years of life through deficits in nurture. This can be the result of emotional neglect, harsh speech, and rejecting behavior. The toxic cocktail might have included chaotic caring and even invited the involvement of child protection services. Then it makes emotional sense to feel worthless. What follows the feeling are the words, "I hate myself" or "I'm bad."

Low self-esteem is clearly a psychological problem but one with spiritual implications. Feeling worthless may result in feelings of shame or guilt—wanting to hide from God. This may be all-pervasive, with a sense of being rejected by the Almighty: "I'm going to hell." It is not hard to see that such early learning might color all subsequent ideas about God. There may be attempts to compensate through overly scrupulous expectations and obsessive practices. Many such examples are seen in pastoral ministry.

The examples of Sally and Nick are also relevant. It would not be surprising if Sally had low self-esteem, since there were few positive messages to her as a child. This would be her legacy regardless of any positive Christian understanding. Nick, on the other hand, felt loved and cared for. A sense of the grace and love of God might come easily to him.

WEEK 1 STUDY GROUP

Pastor Mike is the spiritual leader of a small rural congregation. He suggested the theme of early spirituality for a study group. Initially, he met with a small group of church members who responded to his invitation at a worship service. They came together on a Wednesday night at his home. Mike explained that the group would look at early spiritual formation through a series of exercises. He advised:

> As you do these exercises, try to resist the "enemies" of insight. They include the inner censor (who'll tell you what not to think about) and the inner critic (who'll judge what comes to mind).[26] Try acceptance with both impulses. Say to yourself that the truth will always be friendly to your spiritual growth. After all, Jesus said, "I am the way, the truth, and the life" (John 14:6). These exercises can be the beginning of a new way of seeing yourself, others, and God.

Mike wanted to set the culture of the group as curious and accepting:

> Sometimes we lose the childlike quality of being curious. This is a wonderful guide that can lead us deeper into the spiritual realm.[27] It's spacious, not constricting, as answers can be. What was natural to you as a child? Does the idea of play now seem artificial? What does it feel like to not know?

Mike then said a brief prayer: "Lord, rekindle my curiosity for the journey ahead. I do not need all the answers just yet."

The study group then discussed being curious as children. Mary, an older woman whose husband had died the year before, said with a smile, "I have to think back a few decades. But, as a child, I remember being curious about everything living. Bugs. I kept bringing snails and crawling things back home. [laughing] Mom was not happy!"

Len was in real estate. He had three young children. He planned to alternate coming to the study group with his wife Kylie, "so one of us will stay at home to look after the kids." He recalled, "You'll laugh, but I've always been curious about houses. How people lived and what was important to them. Why do we have what we have? I used to draw house plans and imagine what was in the houses in my street." Others joined in and it was soon obvious that to children the world is a big and mysterious place.

Pastor Mike talked about attachment theory, explaining the four attachment styles. This led to a discussion in which a number of the men acknowledged that they had always been somewhat avoidant in intimate relationships. Stan was in his 50s and had been successful in the finance industry. He and his wife, Cindy, had opted for a "tree change," moved away from the city, and recently joined the congregation. Stan said, "I've always been awkward with my emotions. I remember my father was often away, working, and I was distancing from my mother and sisters. Would my attachment be avoidant?" Cindy exclaimed, "Yes!" It was an anxious moment, but then everyone laughed. Cindy said, "I think I should admit that I've always felt insecure and maybe a little clingy in relationships." It was Stan's turn to agree. Cindy thought, "Then maybe my style is ambivalent?"

Mike explained how our attachment styles might apply to a believer's relationship with God. The group was given Maureen Miner's Attachment to God Questionnaire.[28] He explained, "Answer the questions in this table that relate to your sense of attachment to God. Respond to each statement by indicating how much you agree or disagree with it, using the ratings:"

He added, "To score the responses, add up the scores on each of the aspects of attachment. The higher the score, the more secure the sense of attachment. Scores on each attachment function will range from 3 to 21, and scores on the total scale will range from 12 to 84."

The study group did this for the next ten minutes and then added up their scores. They agreed that the questions were more useful than a raw score. They also noticed differences. Both Stan and Cindy were shocked to find their attachment styles in relationships applied equally to their relationship with God. Pastor Mike had a secure attachment, not necessarily expected in a clergy person, that reflected a very happy but financially insecure childhood. His parents served in the mission field.

Strongly disagree		Mixed/neutral			Strongly agree	
1	2	3	4	5	6	7
1.	In times of difficulty, I seek out God through prayer or Bible reading.					
2.	I reach out to God in times of distress.					
3.	My confidence in God's closeness and responsiveness encourages me to call on Him.					
4.	In times of distress when I turn to God, I find a sense of safety.					
5.	When I felt depressed I would turn to God for comfort and understanding.					
6.	It is God to whom I turn to for aid when distressed.					
7.	God encourages me to go on, climbing up the mountains on the journey of life.					
8.	During challenging times in the past, I trusted that God would be with me.					
9.	Due to feeling God's closeness to me, I took courage to confront life challenges.					
10.	I have cried out to God at times when He seems far away.					
11.	I persist in crying out to God when God seems distant in my troubles.					
12.	When it seems that God has left me, I lament with expectancy of His return.					
Items 1–3:	Attachment function: Proximity seeking					
Items 4–6:	Attachment function: Safe haven					
Items 7–9:	Attachment function: Secure base					
Items 10–12:	Attachment function: Separation protest					

Table 1. Attachment to God questionnaire

The group agreed to remain an open one. People would come when able, and new people were welcome at any time.

SUMMARY

There are many advocates for the importance of early pre-language learning. There is a more general approach in Freud, Jung, and the cognitive unconscious, where the emphasis is placed on unconscious mental processes generally. However, the learning model is more specific. Unconscious learning has been proposed in the research literature with terms such as tacit knowledge, implicit learning, emotional learning, and *habitus*. Attachment theory provides another perspective, again with an extensive research basis. I have used self-esteem to illustrate early learning, but such examples are just the tip of the iceberg. There is little doubt that early learning does help to shape our personality, but does it also influence our spirituality? With the exception of attachment theory, such links have not been widely explored.

Ultimately. the challenge is personal. Each of us will need to return to this wordless realm to find what there is to discover. Only then will it be possible to see the "backstage" of the theater of our lives.

"How?" is the obvious question. You might try some of the exercises used by the study group and add others from the www.earlyspirituality.com website. Experiment with the exercises, especially if you are in ministry. It is best to "try for yourself" in order to explore unconscious spiritual learning before you share any ideas with others.

NOTES

1. There are references to the unconscious throughout his many writings. See James Strachey (ed.), *The standard edition of the complete psychological works of Sigmund Freud*, vols. 1–24, Vintage Press, London, 2001.

2. Drew Westen, "The scientific status of unconscious processes: Is Freud really dead?," *Journal of the American Psychoanalytic Association*, 1999, 47(4):1061–1106.

3. Sally Walters, "Algorithms and archetypes: Evolutionary psychology and Carl Jung's theory of the collective unconscious," *Journal of Social and Evolutionary Systems*, 1994, 17(3):287–306.

4. Ann B. Ulanov and Alvin Dueck, *The living God and our living psyche: What Christians can learn from Carl Jung*, William B. Eerdmans, Grand Rapids, Michigan, 2008; and the popular Robert A. Johnson, *Inner work: Using dreams and active imagination for inner work*, Harper and Row, New York, 1986.

5. John F. Kihlstrom, "The cognitive unconscious," *Science*, 1987, 237(482):1448.

6. Kihlstrom, "The cognitive unconscious," 1450.

7. Kihlstrom, "The cognitive unconscious," 1451.

8. Michael Polanyi, *Personal knowledge*, Routledge and Kegan Paul, London, 1958, 90.

9. Michael Polanyi, *The tacit dimension*, Routledge and Kegan Paul, London, 1967, 4.

10. Arthur S. Reber, *Implicit learning and tacit knowledge: An essay on the cognitive unconscious*, Oxford University Press, New York, 1993, 5.

11. Pierre Bourdieu, *Distinction: A social critique of the judgment of taste,* trans. Richard Nice, Routledge, London, 1984.

12. Bruce Ecker, Robin Ticic, and Laurel Hulley, *Unlocking the emotional brain: Eliminating symptoms at their roots using memory reconsolidation*, Routledge, New York, 2013.

13. Bruce R. Parmenter, *Neo-coherence therapy*, Resource Publications, Eugene, Oregon, 2013.

14. There is a non-conscious dimension in understanding core beliefs.

15. Babette Rothschild, *The body remembers: The psychophysiology of trauma and trauma treatments*, W. W. Norton and Co., New York, 2000, 16.

16. Paul D. MacLean, *The triune brain in evolution*, Plenum Press, New York, 1990.

17. See the chart that contrasts explicit and implicit memory in Rothschild, *The body remembers*, 29.

18. Christopher Bollas, *The shadow of the object: Psychoanalysis of the unthought known*, Free Association Books, London, 1987.

19. Colin, *Human attachment*, has an extensive review of the literature on attachment.

20. The young child is briefly separated from the caregiver in the presence of an observing stranger.

21. Patricia M. Crittendon, "A dynamic-maturational approach to continuity and change in patterns of attachment," in Patricia Crittenden and Angelika H. Claussen (eds), *The organization of attachment relationships: Maturation, culture and context*, Cambridge University Press, Cambridge, 2000, 343–57.

22. Pehr Granqvist, Mario Mikulincer, Vered Gewirtz, and Phillip R. Shaver, "Experimental findings on God as an attachment figure: Normative processes and moderating effects of internal working models," *Journal of Personality & Social Psychology*, 2012, 103(5):804–18.

23. John H. Coe and Todd H. Hall, *Psychology in the spirit: Contours of a transformational psychology*, IVP Academic, Downers Grove, Illinois, 2010, 240–43.

24. Tim Clinton and Joshua Straub, *God attachment: Why you believe, act and feel the way you do about God*, Howard Books, New York, 2010.

25. See the research of Richard L. Bednar, M. Gawain Wells, and Scott R. Peterson, *Self-esteem: Paradoxes and innovations in clinical theory and practice*, American Psychological Association, Washington, D.C., 1989.

26. Helen Cepero, *Journaling as a spiritual practice: Encountering God through attentive writing*, IVP Books, Downers Grove, Illinois, 38. Cepero suggested drawing the inner critic as a stick figure with cartoon balloons for words.

27. Casey Tygrett, *Becoming curious: A spiritual practice of asking questions*, IVP Books, Downers Grove, Illinois, 2017. Tygrett suggests doing a journal of questions, 10.

28. Cited in Bruce A. Stevens and Maureen Minor, *Free to love: Schema therapy for Christians*, Nova Science Publishers, New York, 2017, 16–17; also see Maureen Miner, "Back to the basics in attachment to God: Revisiting theory in light of theology," *Journal of Psychology and Theology*, 2017, 35(2):112–22. There is a questionnaire in Clinton and Straub, *God attachment*, 79–82.

Chapter Two

First Things First

The first cry of the child. Who listens? Well, everyone. An infant is born into a web of relationships: mother, father, siblings, wider family, and possibly carers. I will highlight some important relationships in this chapter.

CARETAKING RELATIONSHIPS

From birth, an infant is flooded with new experiences. Perhaps this is in contrast to the dampened sensations of the fetus *in utero*. The newborn baby seems to be ill-prepared for all the intense sensations from touch, sound, taste, sight, and smell. Hence, the mother or primary carer has an important role in soothing and helping the infant regulate a potentially intense overload of experience. Clearly, infants need carers, both to survive physically and to flourish psychologically.[1]

We enter again a world defined by developmental research, in which psychoanalysis has made a significant contribution.[2] Daniel Stern in *The Interpersonal World of the Infant* identified some of an infant's early precognitive capacities, including a sense of agency, physical and mental cohesion, affectivity, continuity in time, transmitting meaning, having intentions in mind, and a sense of a self that can enter into an intersubjective relationship.[3] Such abilities begin with awareness, but a learning process plays an important role. Perhaps one of the earliest indications of learning is when the baby imitates the behavior of others.[4] Later, we see the emergence of abstract thought, attitudes, expectations in relationships, and goal-related behavior. Such achievements become milestones on the developmental path.

Stern came to some important conclusions. First, he observed how an infant is surrounded by people from birth. Second, the young child can distinguish self and other from the first moments of life. This was important because earlier analysts had seen the infant's perspective in terms of elaborate fantasy. Stern also set the stage for early learning, which is based on the infant's self-in-the-world. This "embeddedness" in the interpersonal world through awareness and participation provides the dynamic elements of what might be identified as a sacred or God-related awareness.

Hence, we can identify early contributing factors to later spiritual development. Here are some:

- *Belonging:* This is an emotional response that includes what Erik Erikson called "basic trust" when people respond to an infant's needs.[5] Attachment theory conceptualizes this in terms of the four attachment patterns. Ideally, this can result in a sense of being at home in the cosmos and feeling at ease in relating to God.
- *Agency*: The infant's earliest perceptions include people and how they act. The interpersonal network includes the self. Self-agency projects to a macro level with a sense of a transcendent agency in God, who can be talked to and who answers prayer.
- *Difference*: This early awareness distinguishes between this and that, big and small, mother and father, perhaps siblings, and eventually develops into areas of spiritual discernment such as the sacred and the profane.

There have been attempts to explore early spiritual awareness. For example, James Loder wrote about the theological significance of the face in infancy.[6] This is more than a literal face and includes a sense of human presence. He explained, "The face is the primal prototype of the religious experience in which one is placed with recognition and affirmation in the context of cosmic order."[7] Jesus, for the Christian, is the face of God.

Roy Steinhoff-Smith applied Stern's research to aspects of faith in infancy (such as developing hope, trust, and love in the first year of life).[8] William Schafer believed that the infant's experience is essentially a spiritual experience.[9] The infant is in touch with presence, joy, and the awareness of others. In optimal circumstances that seems plausible, but infants are also vulnerable to adverse or traumatic experiences. Clearly, early learning, from various sources, will contribute in positive and negative ways to spiritual understanding.

There is a transition at the end of about twelve months, when the baby becomes a toddler and hence more mobile. The carer's role shifts from nurturing, approving, and soothing to become a regulator of socialization who sets limits, saying "No," potentially disapproving and causing pain. Language begins to describe events and to make sense of emotional and sensory experiences.[10] Such are the tributaries of the river of spiritual development.

IMAGINING GOD

Researchers have investigated how young children might imagine God. Psychoanalyst Ana-Maria Rizzuto wrote *The Birth of the Living God*, in which she investigated a range of infantile experiences and concluded, "It is out of this matrix of facts and fantasies, wishes, hopes, and fears, in the exchanges with those incredible beings called parents, that the image of God is concocted."[11] She used the God Questionnaire in her qualitative research. She also looked at children's drawings of God. The results of her study were expressed in psychoanalytic language, but she noted an abundance of spiritual learning from the earliest stages of life. Hans Gunther-Heimbrock also carried out research on children's images of God.[12] Sherry Steenwyck found that more loving and less controlling images of God were associated with life satisfaction among university students.[13]

Through these voices, we can appreciate that a child is open to God through uninhibited spontaneity, imagination, and play. If this is lost in later development, it is not the fault of the child. One advantage of paying attention to early experience is the possibility of regaining what might have been lost.[14]

We have reviewed a number of developmental perspectives on the first year or so of life, but those are but the first steps. James Fowler provided a whole-of-life perspective on faith development that remains influential.[15] We should note that his first stage begins at about three or four years old, so early spiritual learning might be considered more a "pre-stage" of faith.[16] It is important to appreciate the many sources that can potentially make up the emerging image of God.

WEEK 2 STUDY GROUP

After the group settled down, Pastor Mike started a discussion about childhood memories. He asked about family meals. What was eaten? Who prepared the food? Did people talk to each other or eat while watching TV?

Mike introduced the first exercise of the night. He asked those present to make three columns on a page. In the column on the left side, each person listed *age 1*, *age 2* and so on up to *age 12*. Then, in the second column beside the ages, they listed childhood needs at that age. Mike gave an example: *age 1* might include food, shelter, protection, affection, touch, and stimulation. Finally, each person was encouraged to think of a spiritual equivalent for each group of needs and place it in the third column.

Kylie said, "This is easy for me. My youngest is a toddler at 13 months. She has a need for protection. We have a house that provides shelter, being warm or cool as needed. We don't allow her to wander onto a road." Mike agreed with her and added, "The kind of protection changes over the years in developmentally appropriate ways. Now consider your need for protection in the spiritual sense." Kylie thought for a moment and then replied, "I think about your sermons on the Bible. Maybe your teaching protects me from believing the wrong thing?" Mike responded, "Yes, I'd like to think that's true. But I also hope that you feel free, like your daughter, to explore new things. Sometimes that freedom will feel risky, so, spiritually, we need both a sense of protection and the security to find our own truths about God."

Later, Mike asked each member of the group to visualize standing outside a room in their house from childhood. They were to walk in and look around. What did they see? Then they were to choose an object that was meaningful. He continued, "What do you know about this item? Can you tell a story about why it might still be in your possession? Reflect on the gifts you received in your early years. Was there an overall message about how you were valued?"

That night, Sally, like Kylie, was new to the group. She was a college student home for the summer break. Sally remembered a rattle from her infancy. She thought about the noise it made. She used it to get her mother's attention. She saw herself making the noise: "It's fun! I can be free to play." She wondered about how as an adult she has tried to get God's attention, and whether that even made sense with an all-knowing God.

After much discussion, the final exercise for the night was to think back to childhood and recall how God was named. Who talked about God? In what terms? Could this have shaped an early understanding of God? Cindy thought about this:

> I think God was hardly named, perhaps referred to as God, but in a distant kind of way. An object or concept, not a person. There was no warmth or familiarity. There was no appreciation of the many biblical names of God or any understanding of the Trinity. It feels impoverished. Spiritual reality was something in "black and white," but after my conversion it came into color.

Mike concluded with some homework. He said, "Next time we meet, we'll do a genogram. You can google that term and see how to draw the generations in your family. Until next week!"

SUMMARY

I have described the early relational world of the infant. This is based on the reality of carers' responsiveness, not on fantasy. This thesis is informed by Stern and a number of other developmental researchers. It seems likely that early childhood experiences contribute to the formation of faith. This has not been widely investigated, but there are indications in Loder's work on the function of the face and in Rizzuto's work on children's images of God. James Fowler provided a whole-of-life perspective on faith development, although that begins in early childhood and not in infancy. It is apparent that much that is important occurs in the first months and years of life—well before experiences can be remembered or described with words.

We will now move to a broader perspective, which will include some focus on families of origin, intergenerational themes, and culture.

NOTES

1. See the work of Allan N. Schore, *Affect regulation and the repair of the self*, York: W. W. Norton, New York, 2003.

2. Beatrice Beebe and Frank M. Lachmann, *Infant research and adult treatment: Co-constructing interactions*, The Analytic Press, Hillsdale, New Jersey, 2002.

3. Daniel Stern, *The interpersonal world of the infant*, Basic Books, New York, 1985, 7.

4. The role of mimetic interactions is highlighted in the work of René Girard; for example, Wolfgang Palaver, *René Girard's mimetic theory*, trans. Gabriel Borrud, Michigan State University Press, East Lansing, Michigan, 2013.

5. Erik H. Erikson, *Childhood and society*, 2nd ed., Norton, New York, 1963.

6. James Loder, *The logic of the spirit: Human development in a theological perspective*, Jossey-Bass, San Francisco, 1998, 110–11.

7. Loder, *The logic of the spirit*, 91.

8. Roy H. Steinhoff-Smith, "Infancy: Faith before language," in Felicity B. Kelcourse (ed.), *Human development and faith: Life cycle stages of body, mind and soul*, Chalice, St. Louis, 2004, 129–46.

9. William M. Schafer, "The infant as reflection of soul: The time before there was a self," *Zero to Three*, January 2004, 4–8.

10. Rothschild, *The body remembers*, 24.

11. Ana-Maria Rizzuto, *The birth of the living God: A psychoanalytic study*, The University of Chicago Press, Chicago, 1979, 7.

12. Hans Gunther-Heimbrock, "Images and pictures of God: The development of creative seeing [1]," *International Journal of Children's Spirituality*, 1999, 4(1):51–60.

13. Sherry A. M. Steenwyck, David C. Atkins, Jamie D. Bedics, and Bernard E. Whitely Jr., "Images of God as they relate to life satisfaction and hopelessness," *The International Journal for the Psychology of Religion*, 2010, 20:85–96.

14. See Kay L. Northcutt, *Kindling desire for God: Preaching as spiritual direction*, Fortress Press, Minneapolis, Minnesota, 2009, 20.

15. James W. Fowler, *Stages of faith*, Harper and Row, San Francisco, 1981, and *Becoming adult, becoming Christian*, Dove, Blackburn, Victoria, 1984.

16. Fowler considered the pre-stage as not open to empirical investigation; Jeff Astley, "Faith development: An overview," in Jeff Astley and Leslie J. Francis (eds), *Christian perspectives on faith development: A reader*, Gracewing, Leominster, U.K., 1992, xx–xxi.

Chapter Three

From One Generation to the Next

Birth. It is like arriving a few hours late for a party. For me, the "party" started in 1950, decades after most of what was happening in my parents' generation. This leads to an observation of how faith develops over the generations. The genogram is offered as a tool to come to terms with family history. This will help us to recognize what early messages were present and to cast light on unconscious spiritual learning.

When we talk about families, it is always personal, so it will be best if you become involved in drawing your own genogram. This will enable you to identify the family themes that shaped the direction of your life.

THE GENOGRAM

The genogram was developed in family therapy by Murray Bowen. The symbols create a kind of family tree, and the relationship lines indicate "who begat whom."[1] Figure 1 shows what a genogram looks like.

The genogram portrays three generations of Thomas's family. He is married to Amanda and they have two adult children (another, Annette, was stillborn). There are some family problems, which are indicated in the diagram.

Google "genogram" to start doing your own diagram. There are lots of helpful sites. Some will offer software such as *GenoPro* to picture your family on a computer. Fill out the diagram and include members of your family on paper or on your computer. Include your parents, wider family and even more distant relatives. Look over the generations. Can you identify any patterns? You might also identify cultural issues. Look for patterns of migration. Did people value tertiary education or perhaps learning a trade? You might see positive patterns, such as older children looking out for younger siblings.

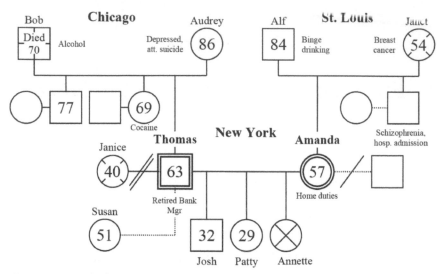

Figure 1.   A genogram

Why are patterns important? Patterns can be the result of common qualities of family members. They can be functional, such as taking responsibility, or negative, through problem behavior such as misusing prescription drugs.

> *Ken* was the oldest son of a farmer. He was expected to take over the family farm, following the example of his father and other males in his family.

In what way was culture embodied in the family? Were customs, distinct traditions, religious practices, views of history, or markers of ethnic identity present? How did the family celebrate? What were special days (birthdays, anniversaries, religious events)? How were values expressed? Was there an honored place for the aged? This provides a context for family life, and it is formative.

Reflect: What expectations were placed on you about how you should live your life? Were you given a life script to follow? Did you feel you were appreciated as a person?

In my own genogram, it was clear that family members often moved to other countries:

> My maternal grandfather came to Australia from New Zealand. My father was born in Boston, Massachusetts, and served in the army in World War 2. He met my mother in Sydney, Australia. After they married, my parents moved to the U.S.A., where I was born. When I was 10 years old, the family returned to Australia. In 1983, I moved with my wife and our children to Boston to do graduate studies and later returned to Australia. I have a younger brother, Mark, who has

lived in the Philippines, Hawaii, mainland U.S.A. and Australia. He married Jo from the Philippines.

Yes, before drawing the genogram I could have said, "People travel in my family." But by doing the work and noticing patterns I came to realize how it typified my experience of family. Travel was part of my early learning. There is a family belief that it is important to take every opportunity—not only to travel but in life! This has been translated into an encouragement to follow our dreams.

The family is our first context. Think about it as an incubator of early learning. Family life includes our first take on everything important: people, relationships, how to live responsibly, to love and be loved.

EARLY LEARNING

Early messages are important. It is not just family patterns: people tell stories. Usually this happens quite spontaneously in family life. What did you hear about your parents and grandparents?

> My father went to World War 2 but only occasionally spoke about his war service. He also talked about how he met my mother in Australia and chose to marry her rather than someone his family had "selected" back in New England, U.S.A. Now my parents are both dead. I am currently collating family photos and I have felt some surprise about how little I know about those pictured.

Think about how the stories reveal the person as "actor." What stories were told about you?

> I would happily amuse myself with picture books as a toddler in my crib or play-pen. My family thought that this was unusual and it generated stories. Indeed, I was to have a lifelong love of books, but it also indicates an avoidant attachment.

There are also emotional themes in families. Marcus Aurelius, the philosopher and emperor of Rome in the second century after Christ, began his *Meditations* acknowledging a debt to family members, including his grandfather, from whom "I learned good morals and the government of my temper," and his father, from whom he learned "modesty and a manly character." Naturally this was not all positive: "from my mother I learned to lose my temper quickly." This theme of emotional inheritance is explored on the *Book of Life* website.[2] What do you consider to be the emotional inheritance you received in your family?

> I had confusing messages from my parents. My father was a dreamer who was good with ideas but lacked something in executing his vision. He hoped for

some kind of commercial success, but it eluded him. My mother was concerned for appearances. She was very attractive in her youth and perhaps that influenced her values. I think I had to find my own way.

Reflect: Would it help to look at your genogram and to use colors to track what emotions were expressed?

TWO SIDES OF THE COIN

There is light and darkness in most families. This is a way to approach negative themes:

> *Abram* came to Australia as a refugee. Many of his near relatives, uncles and aunts died in concentration camps. Even now, in his late 80s, he can hear his parents saying how dangerous the world is: "It only takes one politician to be a Hitler and it could all happen again. Even in Australia . . ." Abram realized that the message about being surrounded by danger and threat was an early learning.

Are there destructive patterns in your family, such as alcohol dependence, gambling, extramarital affairs, or criminal behavior? Also note any problems that repeat through the generations. Each can be a powerful source of early learning.

On a positive note, what strengths do you see? While there may be dysfunctional themes in family life, equally there can be great strengths evident in people. This leads to the many positive qualities that seem natural. For example, most people just cope. This comes from unconscious learning because most people can't *say* exactly how this happens. Consider the following sentences:

- I am worthwhile.
- I am loved and valued by my family.
- I have something of value to contribute.
- My life has meaning.
- The people in my life are dependable.

Those statements all reflect positive early learning, which is derived from positive experiences in the first years, even days, of life: the experiences of being welcomed, loved, and cared for. Just as it is natural for behavior to be triggered by negative hidden learning, it is equally natural to act in healthy ways when such knowing has been positive. And it feels natural and right.

Reflect: Think about your parents and members of your immediate family. List any positive qualities they have, Now go back over the list and tick off any that apply to you as well. Be honest with yourself—this is not a time for false modesty.

> My family members were not emotionally expressive. They were never overtly affectionate, but loving and stable. While I have been critical of some family traits, overall, I am very grateful for my happy childhood and healthy upbringing.

SPIRITUAL REMINISCENCE

Elizabeth MacKinlay and Corrine Trevitt developed the idea of "spiritual reminiscence" and researched it with spiritual reminiscence groups.[3] The groups involved those diagnosed with dementia in residential aged care. A group program was developed with topics such as:

* Life-meaning
* Relationships, isolation, and connecting
* Hopes, fears, and worries
* Growing older and transcendence
* Spiritual and religious beliefs.

The value of spiritual reminiscence has been confirmed in a randomized controlled trial of 106 subjects.[4] The trial demonstrated increases in hope, life satisfaction, and spiritual well-being (through appropriate measures). While MacKinlay and Trevitt's work has been applied to the aged, and it led to an important book on dementia, it is useful for people at any age.[5]

How would you answer the spiritual reminiscence questions? What experiences can you see that have shaped you? Who has influenced your life? What are your most important values? Do you identify as a member of a church or denomination? Can you identify any experiences of God? Did you have an awareness of what might be described as "transcendent"? Do you find the categories suggested by MacKinlay and Trevitt useful? Is this part of your awareness of God?

In my book *The Storied Self: A Narrative Approach to the Spiritual Care of the Aged*, I looked at the important stories of our lives and how they contribute to our sense of identity.[6] I identified a number of undeveloped stories, such as the hidden story before language. Others include the lazy story, the trauma story, the messy story, the body story, the problem story, and the dark story. The God story brings the spiritual realm into focus. The challenge is to find an integrative *deep story* that can be re-authored with new and exciting possibilities. This is a narrative gerontology approach to the care of the aged, but relevant at any age.

EARLY MEMORIES

Our first memory is usually significant. Mine was finger painting in pre-school or kindergarten. Perhaps this predicts some creativity but, sadly, no artistic talent has emerged. A friend, Ann Harvey, recalled:

> I have such a clear memory of a magical moment in my childhood when in Jakarta, at age possibly 4 years, it started to rain. I was outside and from beyond my understanding water droplets fell from the sky. I ran around the yard like an airplane catching water droplets on my tongue shouting "Hujan! Hujan!" my face upturned to the sky. It was a moment of pure joy and I am sure "they [angels] were smiling down at me" from the clouds.

There has been research on first memories.[7] Often, they predict the course of a life in surprising ways. Why is such a memory "chosen" to be so significant as to come out of the fog of early forgetting? Try to recall your first memory and think about whether it has any special meaning.

It is important for each of us to explore our early memories, especially in relation to our spiritual formation. How do we go back? We can simply recall what memories we have:

> I don't remember much from my childhood years. My first spiritual memory was hearing the Christmas carol *Silent Night*. I was in a Christmas pageant in a darkened church sanctuary. It was in the U.S.A., so it must have been before I turned 10 years old. I felt a sense of belonging in this sacred context with both light and darkness.

Also important is an early possession.

> One of the few things my mother kept in her later years (she was very efficient and not sentimental) was a *Reader's Digest* atlas. In the distribution of her "things," after she died, my brother remembered that I often read it. I enjoy maps and exploring the world in distant places. Somehow, I got the message about the world being a big and exciting place. I suspect that this had spiritual implications.

WEEK 3 STUDY GROUP

There was a buzz of excitement as the group gathered. Pastor Mike introduced the genogram. He said, "This is a way of making a diagram of previous generations and seeing family patterns." A number in the group had looked at websites for drawing the genogram and had made a start on drawing their own. Mike explained, "Don't worry about making your diagram neat and tidy; first attempts are always messy."

Monica was new to the group. She had a Scandinavian background: "My parents migrated to the U.S.A., and still speak Swedish at home." She noticed a pattern of religious observance and thought about distinctive family rituals.

Len saw how alcoholism was present in his wider family:

My grandfather was an alcoholic who died from liver problems. I was drinking heavily in my teens until I became a Christian. Now I know it's essential for me to abstain—too many in my family have lost employment or marriages to the bottle.

Mike encouraged the group to include spirituality in their genograms:

Include anything relevant to religious faith in your family. Who was baptized? Who attended church? Did anyone convert to a different religion? Or lose faith? How important was God to those in your family? Who are your models of spiritual maturity? Can you identify anyone with an unhealthy spirituality? What are the effects, both positive and negative, in what you believe or how you have lived? Can you identify religious messages "in the air" of your family when you were young? These can be assumptions relating to your early spiritual formation.

This led to considerable discussion. Monica saw that her parents' faith gave them the courage to come to a new country. Len thought about how his conversion had distanced him from his family, who had long ago abandoned any church attendance:

I think my faith saved me, literally, from self-destruction. But I've been too protective in my withdrawal. I think I should make a special effort at Thanksgiving or Christmas to reconnect and encourage members of my family to think about spiritual values.

This led naturally to a discussion of family heritage. Mike encouraged the group to think about:

What aspects of your family heritage matter to you? Would this include your family name? Your birthplace? Does this anchor you in time and place? What about your culture? How is it important to your spiritual or religious development?

The night ended with a discussion about belonging. Mary thought about how many of her immediate family were now dead, including her husband. She said:

I have children, but they're all a plane ticket away from here. Sadly, my home feels empty at times; everyone important has left. But I feel I belong in my community with great neighbors and here in the church fellowship. It makes a big difference.

Pastor Mike concluded:

We begin in families and generally that's our first place of belonging. This is where we're nurtured in faith and, more generally, life. Some of our later connections are intentional—we choose and when this is reciprocated we have a sense of belonging. All this is part of our spiritual development and faith journey.

Mike also drew the conversation to how our experience of family has shaped us spiritually:

If you think about what you experienced, it's your "normal" and provides clues to early spiritual learning about God. I can hear many indications in what you've shared, but more important is what occurs to you.

Sally asked whether there was any homework for the following week. Mike said, "If you're keen, why not begin to write your autobiography? Notice your emotions as you write it. Focus on any spiritual experiences." Sally said, "Well, I'm on vacation from college. It's good to have an assignment."

SUMMARY

The genogram provides a visual representation of themes that run through the generations of family life. There are indicators of family cohesion or fragmentation, sometimes dark things, and sometimes great strengths. There is much to be noticed. But what is on front stage of the theater of life usually reflects backstage dynamics, such as expectations, family attitudes, religious beliefs, and cultural biases. It is important to notice what might have remained unsaid but was simply expected by people around us, as this provides important clues to a legacy of hidden emotional and spiritual learning.

We will move from this wide lens to a narrower perspective in the chapters that follow.

NOTES

1. See Monica McGoldrick and Randy Gerson, *Genograms in family assessment*, W. W. Norton & Co., New York, 1985.
2. *The Book of Life*: http://www.thebookoflife.org.

3. Elizabeth MacKinlay and Corrine Trevitt, *Facilitating spiritual reminiscence for people with dementia: A learning guide*, Jessica Kingsley Publishers, London, 2015.

4. Li-Fen Wu and Malcolm Koo, "Randomized controlled trial of a six-week spiritual reminiscence intervention on hope, life satisfaction and spiritual well-being in elderly with mild and moderate dementia," *International Journal of Geriatric Psychiatry*, 2016, 31(2):120–27.

5. Elizabeth MacKinlay and Corrine Trevitt, *Finding meaning in the experience of dementia: The place of spiritual reminiscence work*, Jessica Kingsley Publishers, London, 2012.

6. Bruce A. Stevens, *The storied self: A narrative approach to the spiritual care of the aged*, Fortress Academic, Lanham, Maryland, 2018.

7. Carole Peterson, Kelly L. Warren, and Megan M. Short, "Infantile amnesia across the years: A 2-year follow-up of children's earliest memories," *Child Development*, 2011, 82(4):1092–1105.

Chapter Four

The Senses

The five senses, as identified by Aristotle, are sight, touch, hearing, smell, and taste.[1] The senses provide our contact points with reality. Life is experienced.

This is an equation in which experience comes first, not words, but words are helpful to reflect on direct experience: "That smells like a rose," "It tastes like my mother's apple pie," "I can feel soft fur, like a kitten's." Language enables us to think and communicate but is secondary. This chapter introduces research that will provide a scaffolding for understanding early spiritual learning, which, as I will argue, comes through the senses. The way unconscious learning happens will then come into focus.

RESEARCH OPENS DOORS

Perception is best understood as a whole self-activity. Antonio Damasio investigated perception from a neurobiological perspective and identified a process in which signals are processed in the brain.[2] This is an active process in which learning occurs through an encounter with the environment.

This can be further refined. It is too simplistic to assume that our immediate contact with the world is limited to sensations, impressions, sense data, or patterns of stimulation: "rather it is based on the pickup of information. Thus, the function of perception is not the production of experience or representation, but rather the enabling of an organism to function appropriately within its environment."[3] Basically, awareness helps us to survive.

Infants experience their world in recognizable ways. After a review of extensive research data, Tom Bower concluded as follows:

- The infant is built to grasp certain characteristics of the world, mediated by the five senses.
- The infant will detect associations between events.
- These will fit into a predictive framework which might indicate a logical structure.[4]

There are elements of a learning process, since the infant grows in its ability to make appropriate predictions in differing situations. There is also strong evidence that an infant understands contingent relationships between events ("If . . . then" hypotheses).[5] Bower concluded, after reviewing experiments using objects in relation to infants, that "the baby retains an ability to shift between different systems of logic *using the logic that is appropriate to the information given*."[6] It is not just information: there is intelligence.

The question of spiritual experience adds a layer of complexity. At present, clear conclusions are elusive.[7] The brain is complex—to say the least—and its operations can be understood on many levels, from chemical interactions to brain structures. We can observe brain functioning with a variety of brain imaging techniques, including magnetic resonance imaging, but this is an area of research that resists simple answers.[8] There is no "God Spot" or God chemical that explains spirituality.[9] Generally, what have been proposed are models that try to explain the propensity for belief, the effects of religious rituals, and changes in subjective states during an experience such as transcendental meditation. There is some evidence to suggest that some psychoactive chemicals can induce spiritual experiences. There are limits, of course, to such approaches, but these avenues of research hold some promise.[10] For the purposes of this book, I observe that much of the brain's activity is nonconscious.

This does not resolve the mind–body problem. Centuries of discussion have not achieved that.[11] Descartes' error was his dualism, separating body from mind with his *res extensa* and *res cogitans*. Nancy Murphy, a leading theologian, has concluded that "We are bodies—there is no additional metaphysical element such as mind or soul or spirit . . . this 'physicalist' position need not deny that we are intelligent, moral and spiritual."[12] While there is some danger of reductionism, an embodied selfhood is no barrier to sociality, to attaining heights of reflective thought, to being sustained by deep emotions and motivation, or to developing spiritually in a relationship with God.[13] A recent development is the idea of embodied cognition, which offers a better alternative to the dualistic perspective.[14] This has also been applied to understanding religion and spirituality.[15]

Mark Wynn has explored people's spiritual sensibility, as distinguished from religious belief.[16] There has been a common misunderstanding that relating to God is "otherworldly" and is assisted by turning away from the sensory world.[17] Again, this presents a false dualism. We can recognize interaction. Wynn believed that having a religious viewpoint changes what we see. For example, a religious conversion can potentially enliven the sensory world through the purging of certain egocentric kinds of attachment.[18] There can be a gradual shift in perception, perhaps incremental: "These things now serve to image God in some measure—since their glory is in some fashion an echo of the divine glory."[19] This comes, potentially, through all the senses.

Perhaps more helpful is research on consciousness. We have only begun to understand that phenomenon, but what we know suggests that the brain has such a capacity, although we are largely ignorant of the mechanism. It is about our body-as-self, as Stephen Crites has observed that only the self as a whole can be understood to be acting in stories.[20] We all have a sense of self, although we cannot fully grasp it.[21]

This discussion brings to the same table our five senses, the ways we interact with reality, neurobiological pathways, consciousness, and spiritual awareness. Nothing has been fully resolved, but with these very different voices perhaps a conversation is possible.

THE SENSES

The Bible records the divine human encounter in terms of the senses. The assumption is that all are involved: "hear the word of the Lord" (Isaiah 1:10);[22] "the pure in heart . . . they will see God" (Matthew 5:8); "O, taste and see that the Lord is good!" (Psalms 34:8); the faithful "spreads in every place the fragrance that comes from knowing him" (2 Corinthians 2:14). Indeed, the original witnesses to the resurrection testified that "we have seen with our eyes, what we have looked at and touched with our own hands, concerning the word of life" (1 John 1:1). Perhaps we can appreciate how seriously God takes the material world (Colossians 2:9).

The expression "spiritual senses" (*sensus spiritales*) first occurred in the Latin translation of Origen of Alexandria (c. 185–c. 254 AD).[23] This came to be systematized in Western medieval theology in relation to vision, audition, olfaction, touch, and taste, usually by a reference such as "ears of faith" or "eyes of the soul." Paul Gavrilyuk and Sarah Coakley have argued for the continuing relevance of the senses in the theological tradition. But they also acknowledge difficulties, since God is essentially a being who is unlike us and inherently mysterious: "we look not at what can be seen but to what cannot be seen" (2 Corinthians 4:18).[24] This will prove to be an unresolved tension.

Perhaps there is a theological way forward. In the incarnation, the Son of God became "fully human," which unites the senses and links to an awareness of the divine.[25] This also gives shape to the divine–human relationship.[26] This is the theological interchange that matters: God coming as "one of us" implies that we have a natural ability to respond to God. Everything that is human belongs, including our senses.

The Bible and the Christian tradition portray a faith that is experienced. Over the centuries, people have received visions, revelations, spiritual insights, and other communications from the divine realm, but the focus has been more on the content than on analyzing the cognitive means of "getting the message." Gavrilyuk and Coakley chart the *sensus spiritales* tradition in the Christian church.[27]

Augustine, for example, in his *Confessions*:

> I have learnt to love you late, Beauty [God] at once so ancient and so new! . . . You called me, you cried aloud to me; you broke my barrier of deafness. You shone upon me; your radiance enveloped me; you put my blindness to flight. You shed your fragrance about me; I drew breath and now I gasp for your sweet odor. I tasted you, and now I hunger and thirst for you. You touched me, and I am inflamed with love of your peace.[28]

More recently, in the twentieth century, Hans Urs von Balthasar[29] incorporated the senses into his theological aesthetics in *The Glory of the Lord*.[30] Beauty must take a form (*Gestalt*), which is Jesus Christ for the Christian. In this, both sensory and suprasensory dimensions are required.[31] Some would caution against an overreliance on the senses. Some mystics have walked the *via negative*, turning away from any representation of God. Many have argued that there is a risk of idolatry, hence justifying iconoclastic tendencies such as rejecting images, including touching a statue or smelling incense. In some reformed circles, hearing the word of God—effectively using only one sense—has been elevated to be the divinely sanctioned source of truth. Von Balthasar is an important corrective to any bias against the senses in some Christian circles.

For me, the existence of God is something I assume as a believer, I hope not uncritically but as a personal reality who can be experienced through meditation, reading the Bible, being open to transcendence and mystery, attending worship, and prayer. This accords with my limited experience. It is like an appreciation of beauty, so my heart—though less extravagant—is at one with Augustine's.

Ola Sigurdson in *Heavenly Bodies* made the point that:

> . . . neither theology nor philosophy gets at the body as theme and phenomenon in the human-life world other than through an interpretation of the pre-theoretical

—if not pre-linguistic!—conceptions and experiences of the body that find expression in these texts and practices.[32]

This accords with my view that we learn about God through direct experience and that this learning takes place through the senses. This process is initially noncognitive or unconscious. And, often, so it remains. The quest is to bring such learning into awareness and faithfully live with such insight.

We learn about God through such modes of experience. Recently, I saw the beautiful *The Lady and the Unicorn* tapestries from the Musée de Cluny (which were on exhibition in Australia). These glorious sixteenth-century works illustrate the five senses and allow for a sixth sense, or an overall focus, labeled *Mon Seul Désir* (my sole desire).[33] For me, the exhibition was a wonderful foretaste of what I anticipate as a beatific vision—the eschatological hope of the believer in Christ (Revelations 1:12–16).

It is not possible to resolve the philosophical or theological problems of how a believer might experience God through his or her senses—or even whether another spiritual sense is needed. That is a "bone" for others to "chew." But, clearly, the senses are the way we contact reality, and it makes sense that this will apply to the spiritual realm as well.

IMPLICIT LEARNING AND THE SENSES

Unconscious learning and the senses can now be drawn together. While implicit learning has a long history in academic research, it has not been defined in a universally accepted way. I have cited Arthur Reber's definition, but it is worth observing that implicit learning occurs unintentionally and automatically and results in knowledge that is difficult to put into words.[34]

Studies in implicit learning have included the learning of an artificial grammar, sequences, and probability estimates. There are thousands of published studies. Generally, the idea is to demonstrate that a participant in an experiment has gained relevant information without being able to verbalize that knowledge. There are important controversies in this area of research that are beyond my scope here.[35] There has also been research about possible underlying cognitive processes based in neuroscience, but *what* remains an open question.[36] There is also research that demonstrates that implicit learning happens throughout the human life span. Indeed, early learning can be most effective in certain areas, such as a second language, some sports, and playing musical instruments.[37] There is evidence that implicit learning happens through various senses.[38] This includes the visual,[39] odor,[40] hearing,[41] sense of the body,[42] and movement.[43]

There are important implications. Reber drew on evolutionary theory to argue that consciousness is a relatively recent arrival, with the implication that it was built upon deeper and more primitive brain processes and structures that functioned independently of awareness. Those processes and structures show different properties from those more recently evolved: "[O]ne of these is that structures with greater antiquity tend to be more robust and resilient, less prone to disruption of function than the newer."[44] Implicit learning is foundational, and it is even more surprising that any function is conscious rather than unconscious.[45] There are advantages, as Marvin Chun and Yuhong Jiang have noted that implicit learning allows more information to be acquired than is possible through consciously mediated channels.[46] This information has greater utility because such mechanisms operate outside of awareness to influence and control behavior.[47] It is also likely that something learned in this way is better retained and more robust in the face of neurological injury.[48]

There is an important qualification that can be made at this point. Something may have been learned but not necessarily remembered. Memory involves taking in, storing, and retrieving. A break at any point in this process will mean that something is not recalled.

Memory is an enormous area of research. Commonly, a distinction is made between "episodic" and "autobiographical" memory, the first being more of an event and the second placed within a sense of unfolding personal history. Both might be considered "declarative" memory as opposed to implicit memory, which is acquired in a nonconscious way and includes procedural memory or "how to" do something.[49] Such a memory is not accompanied by an internal sensation of the event or of being remembered.[50] Memory is of course related to learning and also shows many of the distinctions that have been made for learning.

Implicit learning has an important role in human functioning. Arguably, this is the most important learning. We have seen that it has a wide reach, incorporates more than can be consciously assimilated, influences action, is more robust, and resists change. It seems plausible that this is how unconscious spiritual learning occurs, which has implications for our spiritual formation.

WEEK 4 STUDY GROUP

Pastor Mike did not need any icebreakers for the next study group meeting. Everyone was now used to participating. When he asked about first memories, most people were able to recall something. Kylie said, "I think this is my first memory. I'm in a pram and looking up at light coming through leaves. There's a play of light and shadows made by the breeze." Cindy had a memory in church: "I remember the sound of an organ. Real pipes, which could thunder at times, then play a sweet melody on the high notes." After everyone had shared, Mike noted, "Sometimes our first memories are like a trajectory, indicating a direction our life might take. Can you make any connections through your first memory?" Cindy smiled: "Well, music has always been important. I went to the conservatory to study the flute and I've taught music all my life. It's weird that my first memory would 'predict' this!"

Mike then introduced an exercise. He explained that our early learning is through the five senses:

Imagine that you've arrived at your holiday destination. It's a beach resort. What's your first reaction?

- Do you feel of the sand under your feet, the warmth of the sun on your skin, or a cool sea breeze on your face?
- Do you hear the waves breaking or notice the sound of seagulls or the rustling of leaves in the wind?
- Do you enjoy the view of the beach, the blue sea, and the movement of people?
- Are you drawn to the smell of the sea or the flowers and trees around?
- Are you looking for exotic dining with new dishes to try out?

What's the first thing you notice at the resort?[51]

The group offered a variety of responses. Mary said, "I first look and see the ocean." Stan offered, "I feel the warmth of sun on my face. It's really relaxing." His wife Cindy added, "I hear the sound of the waves breaking." Sally was drawn to the smells. No one had taste as their first choice.

Mike said, "It is possible that this exercise shows which sense we 'prefer.' Maybe we think in terms of 'first' and 'second' choices. Later, we'll see that this might be important for how we experience God."

Mike then asked about their first spiritual memory:

What do you notice about this memory? Do you see a God representation or a sacred image, such as a stained-glass window? Do you visualize a place? Hear music or another sound, such as drums? Smell cooking or incense? Taste the sacrament or food associated with religious people gathering. Do you feel a handshake or a hug? Or do you experience this memory through more than a single sense?

Cindy said, "The organ music was both my first memory and also my first religious memory. Does that say something?" Mike thought for a moment, "I'm not sure. Maybe. What do you think?" Cindy said, "I think it reinforces the importance of my early faith experiences."

Later, Sally asked Pastor Mike if he would assign a focus for the week ahead. He said:

> The input from all the senses is varied, complex, and rich in association. This is the environment of early unconscious learning. Life is learned by answering questions such as: Do I belong? Am I loved? Is this a safe place? Do I feel secure? What interests me? This is a smorgasbord of early learning laying a foundation for life. Each also provides the building blocks for a sense of God. Think about the messages in early life. What's still with you? Make a list. Next week, we'll look more closely at the faith implications of the five senses. For the next meeting, can everyone bring two or three childhood photos?

SUMMARY

The senses are the way we experience reality. Indeed, they are the avenues of early learning. The importance of unconscious learning has been established in infant and early childhood research. This is supported by Reber's work on implicit learning. We can also conclude that learning tends to be holistic; the dualistic separation of the mind and body is a dead end. Theologian Mark Wynn has argued for the unity of spiritual perception. The importance of the individual senses for perceiving God is seen in the writings of Augustine, von Balthasar and Coakley. But this does not fully resolve the problem of God being almost totally unlike us. While this chapter has been somewhat theoretical, it provides a basis for the later chapters on the individual senses.

NOTES

1. The five senses were first proposed by Aristotle; *De Anima*, Book 3. Commentary by Ronald Polansky, *Aristotle's De Anima*, Cambridge University Press, Cambridge, U.K., 2007, 361–79.

2. Antonio R. Damasio, *Descartes' error: Emotion, reason and the human brain*, Avon Books, New York, 2005, 224.

3. Malika Auvray and Charles Spence, "The multisensory perception of flavor," *Consciousness and Cognition*, 2008, 17:1016–31, at 1025.

4. T. G. R. Bower, *The rational infant: Learning in infancy*, W. H. Freeman and Co., New York, 1989, 78–79.

5. Bower, *The rational infant*, 93.

6. Bower, *The rational infant*, 123 (emphasis in the original).

7. An overview is in David B. Yaden, Jonathan Iwry, and Andrew B. Newberg, "Neuroscience and religion: Surveying the field," in Niki K. Clements (ed.), *Mac-*

Millan *interdisciplinary handbooks on religion: The brain, cognition and culture*, 277–99, MacMillan, New York, 2016.

8. For example, Dimitrios Kapogiannis, Aron K. Barbey, Michael Su, Giovanna Zamboni, Frank Krueger, and Jordan Grafman, "Cognitive and neural foundations of religious belief," *Proceedings of the National Academy of Sciences of the U.S.A.*, 2009, 106(12):4876–81.

9. Yaden et al., "Neuroscience and religion," 286.

10. Andrzej K. Jastrzebski, "The neuroscience of spirituality: An attempt at critical analysis," *Pastoral Psychology*, 2018, 67:515–24. It is too early to talk about developing a neurotheology.

11. For example, the influential Michel Foucault, *History of madness*, Jean Khalfa (ed.), trans. Jonathan Murphy and Jean Khalfa, Routledge, London, 2006, 211.

12. Nancy Murphy, *Bodies and souls, or spirited bodies?*, Cambridge University Press, Cambridge, U.K., 2006, ix. It seems likely that the original Hebrew understanding of person as a whole being was closer to a physicalist view, although it is possible that there is more than one view in the New Testament.

13. Murphy, *Bodies and souls*, 146–47. For further discussion on a neuroscience basis, see Jesse L. Preston, Ryan S. Ritter, and Justin Hepler, "Neuroscience and the soul: Competing explanations for the human experience," *Cognition*, 2012, online: http://dx.doi.org/10.1016/j.cognition.2012.12.003.

14. Lucia Foglia and Robert A. Wilson, "Embodied cognition," *WIREs Cognitive Science*, 2013, 4:319–25.

15. Tamer M. Soliman, Kathryn A. Johnson, and Hyunjin Song, "'It's not all in your head': Understanding religion from an embodied cognition perspective," *Perspectives on Psychological Science*, 2015, 10(6):852–64.

16. Mark R. Wynn, *Renewing the senses: A study of the philosophy and theology of the spiritual life*, Oxford University Press, Oxford, 2013.

17. Wynn, *Renewing the senses*, 8.

18. Wynn, *Renewing the senses*, 26.

19. Wynn, *Renewing the senses*, 48.

20. "Neither disembodied minds nor mindless bodies can appear in stories. There the self is given whole, as an activity in time." Stephen Crites, "The narrative quality of experience," *Journal of the American Academy of Religion*, 1971, 39(3):309.

21. Sarah Coakley, "Introduction: Religion and the body," in Sarah Coakley (ed.), *Religion and the body*, Cambridge University Press, Cambridge, U.K., 1997, 3. Complexity is seen in Bryan S. Turner, "The body in Western society: Social theory and its perspectives," in Coakley, *Religion and the body*, 15–41.

22. All quotes are from the New Revised Standard Version.

23. Paul L. Gavrilyuk and Sarah Coakley (eds.), *The spiritual senses: Perceiving God in Western Christianity*, Cambridge University Press, Cambridge, U.K., 2012, 2.

24. Gavrilyuk & Coakley, *The spiritual senses*, 1–2.

25. Gavrilyuk & Coakley, *The spiritual senses*, 18.

26. Ola Sigurdson, *Heavenly bodies: Incarnation, the gaze, and embodiment in Christian theology*, trans. Carl Olsen, William B. Eerdmans, Grand Rapids, Michigan, 2016, 148.

27. Gavrilyuk & Coakley, *The spiritual senses*, with contributions from various scholars.

28. R. S. Pine-Coffin, trans., *St. Augustine Confessions*, Penguin Books, Harmondsworth, Middlesex, U.K., 1961, Book 10, 27, 231–32.

29. See overview of Mark J. McInroy, "Karl Rahner and Hans Urs von Balthasar," in Gavrilyuk & Coakley, *The spiritual senses,* 257–74.

30. An accessible way into his work is Medard Kehl and Wemer Loser (eds), *The von Balthasar reader*, Crossroad Herder, New York, 1982.

31. McInroy, "Karl Rahner and Hans Urs von Balthasar," 272.

32. Sigurdson, *Heavenly bodies,* 36.

33. Elisabeth Delahaye, *The lady and the unicorn*, Réunion des musées nationaux, Paris, 2007.

34. Christopher M. Conway and David B. Pisoni, "Neurocognitive basis of implicit learning of sequential structure and its relation to language processing," *Annals of the New York Academy of Sciences*, 2008, 1145:113.

35. An example highlighting issues is Peter A. Frensch and Dennis Runger, "Implicit learning," *Current Directions in Psychological Science*, 2003, 12(1):13–18.

36. Conway & Pisoni, "Neurocognitive basis of implicit learning," 123.

37. And this has been connected with more primitive parts of the brain. Karolina Janacsek, Józcef Fiser, and Dezso Nemeth, "The best time to acquire new skills: Age-related differences in implicit sequence learning across the human lifespan," *Developmental Science*, 2012, 15(4):496–505.

38. Conway & Pisoni, "Neurocognitive basis of implicit learning," 113–31. It can also transfer across the various senses, 114.

39. Marvin M. Chun and Yuhong Jiang, "Contextual cueing: Implicit learning and memory of visual context guides spatial attention," *Cognitive Psychology*, 1998, 36:28–71.

40. For example, Joachim Degel, Dag Piper, and Egon P. Köster, "Implicit learning and implicit memory for odors: The influence of odor identification and retention time," *Chemical Senses*, 2001, 26(3):267–80.

41. Christopher M. Conway, David B. Pisoni, Esperanza M. Anaya, Jennifer Karpicke, and Shirley C. Henning, "Implicit sequence learning in hearing children and deaf children with cochlear implants," *Research on Spoken Language Processing*, 2008, 29:24–53.

42. Matthew R. Longo and Patrick Haggard, "An implicit body representation underlying human position sense," *Proceedings of the National Academy of Sciences of the U.S.A.*, 2010, 107(26):11727–32.

43. Miriam Reiner, "Sensory cues, visualization and physics learning," *International Journal of Science Education*, 2009, 31(3):343–64.

44. Reber, *Implicit learning*, 8.

45. Reber, *Implicit learning*, 10.

46. Chun & Jiang, "Contextual cueing," 30.

47. Chun & Jiang, "Contextual cueing," 66.

48. Diane C. Berry, "How implicit is implicit learning?," in Geoffrey Underwood (ed.), *Implicit cognition*, Oxford University Press, Oxford, 1995, 218–19.

49. There is enormous research on memory of all kinds. See, for example, Martin A. Conway, "Memory and the self," *Journal of Memory and Language*, 2005, 35(1):594–628; and Daniel L. Schacter and Henry L. Roediger, "Implicit memory: History and current status," *Journal of Experimental Psychology: Learning, Memory and Cognition*, 1987, 13(1):501–18.

50. Clinton & Straub, *God attachment*, 55.

51. This has been adapted from "NLP representational systems test," *Excellence Assured*, online: http://excellenceassured.com/nlp-training/nlp-preferred-representational-systems-test.

Chapter Five

Sight

Now to examine the individual senses. This will help us to appreciate both early capacities and their implications for spiritual awareness. First, sight.

INFANT AWARENESS

The infant is visually curious from birth. She will look toward a light source or away if the light is too intense. Within days or weeks, she will reach for objects, indicating a sense of depth.[1] Indeed, "The more the perceptual world of the young infant is investigated the more competent the infant seems to be."[2] Kristin Hartshorn and Carolyn Rovee-Collier also demonstrated infant learning with a range of experiments.[3] It has been shown that infants have automatic implicit learning through sight[4] and that contextual cues are important.[5]

There is a rapid development in the infant's social sensitivity. This includes being able to respond to gender cues and imitating behavior.[6] There are also signs of self-efficacy, in which her behavior results in getting her needs met.[7] We have noticed that getting Mother's attention is part of this process. Infants learn and transfer this understanding to novel situations—thus demonstrating intelligence.[8]

The young infant is usually interested in and responsive to people. A newborn can imitate facial expressions.[9] Visual stimulation brings a quick response. Think about an infant delighting in a game of peek-a-boo. There is a profound reciprocity in such interactions. There is also a sense in which the child sees herself through the response of the carer. Donald Winnicott called this "the looking glass self."[10]

Gradually, a child is attracted to things. This is a precursor of what will later develop into a sense of beauty. This, too, is often associated with sight:

we see something interesting and later realize that it is also beautiful. Modern aesthetic theories highlight features of aesthetic experience, such as that it can be revelatory, transformative, and participatory.[11]

CHRISTIAN SEEING

Faces are important. This was highlighted by James Loder's work on the significance of the face in infancy. The face is "naked" in relationships. Apparently, we need only five facial muscles to survive, but we have forty-three muscles to reveal our inner selves. This is to express what was conveyed in *panim,* the Hebrew word for face, which means not just face but presence and the wholeness of being.[12] The face of God, we believe, is turned toward us. This is recalled in the familiar blessing "The Lord bless you and keep you; the Lord make his face to shine upon you." (Numbers 6:24–25). More specifically for the Christian, this is expressed in our understanding of Jesus Christ revealed in the New Testament.

The glory of God is evident to sight: "The heavens are telling the glory of God and the firmament proclaims his handiwork" (Psalms 19:1). But there is seeing and not-seeing. God is described as invisible (Colossians 1:15, John 5:37, 1 Timothy 1:17). Indeed, the Almighty is beyond not just sight but understanding. We have almost no conception of the created universe, in which distance is measured in light years, let alone the Creator. Traditionally, there is a distinction between kataphatic and apophatic approaches to God. The positive or kataphatic way uses images, ideas, symbols, and language to enhance a relationship with God. It is a mediated seeing. The negative or apophatic way is a path of unknowing toward the mysteries of God, as proposed by Pseudo-Dionysius.[13] We can choose the way of light or the way of darkness.

But is such a choice necessary? Sigurdson has written about the believer's gaze acknowledging the inherent contradiction of "looking at the invisible."[14] But the visible and the invisible are not rivals. They are connected, just as transcendence and immanence are a dynamic unity.[15] There is also God in Christ through the incarnation, not that we can literally see the human Christ, but the apostles did and this has implications for relating to God that can never be reduced to a purely cognitive level.[16]

While there is a contradiction in any possibility of seeing God, there is a long tradition in the church of *visio divina* or holy seeing. For example, ritual may be thought of as an embodiment of the human–divine relationship and presented to our visual sense.[17] But images of God? Some would assert that this is against the Old Testament commandment "You shall not make for yourself an idol, whether in the form of anything that is in heaven above, or that is on the earth beneath . . ." (Exodus 20:4). Some translations refer to "graven images," but what is being rejected? Could it be pagan idolatry? Of course, there have been many times in the history of the church in which iconoclastic forces have prevailed.[18] However, talent has been valued from the beginning of our faith, and artists such as Bezalel are mentioned in the Bible (Exodus 31:1–5).

There is also a long theological tradition acknowledging artistic representations of the sacred. Almost every significant theologian in the history of the church has had something to say on the topic, usually seeing benefit for the believer.[19] Hans Urs von Balthasar (d. 1988), a leading twentieth-century theologian, argued that the aesthetic experience is like a religious experience and works in a similar way to how theology proceeds. Arguably, his major work is the many volumes of his systematics comprising the trilogy of *The Glory of the Lord, Theo-logic* and *Theo-drama.*[20] Beauty is seeing the good, the beautiful, and the true. This leads to a "holy worldliness."[21] Beauty in the human realm provides an analogy with divine beauty and is already shaped by the divine beauty in the incarnation.[22] Our response is delight. I see the importance of this for doing theology that is not totally dependent on rational thinking.

Most churches today have works of art in some form: stained-glass windows, tapestries, wood carvings for the altar or holy table, sacred furniture, high ceilings to invoke awe, decorated candles, and sometimes statues, icons, mosaics, and works of art.

Icons are important in some traditions and provide an example of a sacred art. They portray the best possible models for Christian life and may encourage the believer to see through a "door" into the company of heaven. Icons also encourage the viewer to open himself or herself to God.[23] Learning to read an icon tutors in a language of reflection, meditation, symbol, and prayer. There are no shadows in an icon because the light comes from within the holy person. The enlarged eyes show the soul, there are large ears to hear the Word of God, and there is a small mouth to indicate that the less said, the better. Sober faces indicate the reality of life, the two fingers on Christ show that he is being divine and human, and so on.[24] Paul used the word "icon" to describe Jesus Christ as the exact image (Greek *eikōn* = English *image*) of the invisible God (Colossians 1:15).

Some Christians will paint an icon as part of their devotional life. Traditionally, this is called *writing* an icon. Workshops teach the theological language of icons. This is a disciplined approach to visualizing Jesus or Mary or God. You can google "icons" and see some of what has been created in the Christian tradition over the centuries. Leading theologian Sarah Coakley has a profound discussion of this in her book, *God, Sexuality and the Self,* including a section on Andrei Rublev's famous 1411 icon of the Trinity.[25]

It is based on the three visitors to Abraham. The picture invites you to join them at the table.

You might consider talking to someone of the Orthodox Church about how they see icons. Have you visited an Orthodox Church and seen the abundance of icons? There is a sense of being surrounded by the saints.

While there are some Christian traditions that value simplicity, most will have some visual markers, such as a cross or a verse of scripture on the wall. If none of this appeals, the believer can turn to the world outside, where God's "fingerprints" are obvious.

An appreciation of the visual is important theologically. There has been a surge in interest in theological aesthetics, or aesthetic theology, over the past few decades.[26] Humanity is in the image of God, which reaches an apex in the person of Jesus Christ. If we believe in the incarnation, God will be seen through Christ and less transparently in humanity in general: "A faith based on the divine incarnation will eventually find expression in the realm of the visible."[27] There is also the Christian hope of one day seeing God in heaven.

SUMMARY

Sight is perhaps our most important link to reality. We look. It is an active process.[28] After birth, we get our first sight of the world of objects and people and, ultimately, see indications of the transcendent, including God. This is an important pathway for unconscious learning, which includes learning about the sacred realm. It highlights one of the mechanisms through which early learning occurs. This, too, needs to be appreciated at a personal level. Experiential exercises can help us to rediscover our early impressions. Go to www. earlyspirituality.com for some suggestions.

NOTES

1. Bower, *The rational infant*, 13–15.

2. Bower, *The rational infant*, 24.

3. Kristin Hartshorn and Carolyn Rovee-Collier, "Infant learning and long-term memory at 6 months: A confirming analysis," *Developmental Psychology*, 1997, 30(1):71–85.

4. Nicholas B. Turk-Browne, Justin A. Jungé, and Brian Scholl, "The automaticity of visual statistical learning," *Journal of Experimental Psychology*, 2005, 134(4):552–64.

5. Annabelle Goujon, André Didierjean, and Simon Thorpe, "Investigating implicit statistical learning mechanisms through contextual cueing," *Trends in Cognitive Sciences*, 2015, 19(9):524–33.

6. Bower, *The rational infant*, 125–47.

7. Bower, *The rational infant*, 145–46.

8. Bower, *The rational infant*, 150.

9. Bower, *The rational infant*, 31.

10. Donald W. Winnicott, "Mirror role of the mother and family in child development," in *Playing and Reality*, Routledge, London, 2005, 149–59.

11. Oleg V. Bychkov, "Introduction," in Oleg V. Bychkov and James Fodor (eds), *Theological aesthetics after von Balthasar*, Routledge, New York, 2008, xii.

12. Adele Ahlberg Calhoun, *Spiritual disciplines handbook: Practices that transform us*, revised edition, IVP Books, Downers Grove, Illinois, 2015, 159.

13. Tom Ryan, SM, "Our pathway to God: Sight," *Compass*, Summer 2014, 48(4):16.

14. Sigurdson, *Heavenly bodies*, 258.

15. Sigurdson, *Heavenly bodies*, 271.

16. Sigurdson, *Heavenly bodies*, 35.

17. Sigurdson, *Heavenly bodies*, 284.

18. There was a Reformed reaction to the medieval use of visual imagery. See discussion in William Dyrness, *Reformed theology and visual culture*, Cambridge University Press, Cambridge, U.K., 2004.

19. For a comprehensive survey of primary sources, see Gesa Elsbeth Thiessen (ed.), *Theological aesthetics: A reader*, William B. Eerdmans, Grand Rapids, Michigan, 2004.

20. Hans Urs von Balthasar published extensively between 1961 and 1985. The most accessible way into his thought is Medard Kehl and Wemer Loser (eds), *The von Balthasar reader*, Crossroad Herder, New York, 1982.

21. Aidan Nichols, "Introduction," Hans U. Von Balthasar, *Mysterium Paschale: The mystery of Easter*, trans. Aidan Nichols, Ignatius Press, San Francisco, 1990, 4.

22. George Pattison, "Is the time right for a theological aesthetics?," in Oleg V. Bychkov and James Fodor (eds), *Theological aesthetics after von Balthasar*, 107–14, Ashgate, Aldershot, U.K., 2008, 109–10.

23. See Cornelia A. Tsakiridou, *Icons in time, persons in eternity: Orthodox theology and the aesthetics of the Christian image*, Ashgate, Farnham, U.K., 2012.

24. Calhoun, *Spiritual disciplines handbook*, 63–64.

25. Sarah Coakley, *God, sexuality and the self: An essay 'on the Trinity'*, Cambridge University Press, Cambridge, U.K., 2013, 190–265.

26. Pattison, "Is the time right for a theological aesthetics?," 107.

27. Aidan Nichols, O.P. *Redeeming beauty: Soundings in sacral aesthetics*, Ashgate, Aldershot, U.K., 2007, 21.

28. Sigurdson, *Heavenly bodies*, 152.

Chapter Six

Touch (Including the Sense of Body)

We are embodied. Of course, this is obvious. Our experience of the world is mediated by our material selves. After birth, we are lifted up, held, nurtured, and protected. Healthy touch leads to feeling secure in relationships, being protected and "at home." Some families are physically expressive and show abundant affection. Others, while still loving, are more reserved. Both are "styles" of loving; the important factor is feeling loved (regardless of how). Donald Winnicott developed this with his idea of nurturing, usually maternal, as a "holding environment."[1]

Like sight, the sense of touch is important at all levels. It is communication without words. And it is important spiritually, as we will see in this chapter.

EMBODIED

The body is present in every sense of the word. The philosopher Paul Ricoeur noted that our body opens us up to the world in two ways:

- The sense organs to experience and for action in the world.
- The body as a surface at which we are exposed to the scrutiny of others.[2]

We can note that "the body is a pre-conceptual presence which accompanies all our intentional entanglements in the world. By means of the body we take part in a shared world."[3] The body expresses individuality. It also functions as a boundary marking inside and outside, here and there, me and you. Bodily, we occupy a place in time and space.

The body is the physical sensor that receives information. This happens through two systems:

- the exteroceptive, which responds to stimuli outside the body
- the interoceptive, which responds to internal stimuli.

An external event will register at the two levels. For example, seeing a lion, even in a zoo behind bars, might lead to an increase in heart rate. Inside and outside stimuli come together at the sight of the wild animal.

The body might be important to how we understand language. For example, language's origins may be gestural (movements of the body, expressions of the human face, and intonations of vocalizations that provide the primitive framework for language).[4] Hands and mouths "grasp," so it could be argued that cognition as a mental mode of grasping arises from the physical act of grasping.

The body is where we register our emotions. Babette Rothschild outlined how emotions are felt in the body: anger (muscular tension, especially in the jaw and shoulders), sadness (wet eyes, a lump in the throat), disgust (nausea), happiness (deep breathing, sighing), fear (racing heart, trembling), and shame (rising heat, particularly to the face).[5] This leads to the larger question of awareness.

Meditation and mindfulness have become increasingly popular. Both are ways to become more self-aware. Meditation can be thought of as an umbrella term for a range of practices to achieve a desired consciousness. Mindfulness is the act of focusing on present experience. Meditation in this sense is a type of meditation alongside tantra, yoga, sexuality, silence, breathing, and emptiness.[6] Jon Kabat-Zinn, one of the popularizers of mindfulness, defined it as "paying attention in particular ways: on purpose, in the moment, and non-judgmentally."[7] Mindfulness is simply sustained attention and can include an intense awareness of the body, for example with a focus breath.

My daughter, Naomi, who trained in clinical psychology, is enthusiastic about a therapeutic technique called "focusing." This originated in the research of Eugene Gendlin, who encouraged sustained attention on unclear sensations.[8] Focusing is a natural skill that can be observed in people of all cultures, but in our cognitive Western culture many seem to have lost the ability:

> *Harry* was encouraged by his pastoral counsellor to attune to the felt sense of the jittery sensation in his stomach and a heaviness when he thought about his wife, who was terminally ill. He found that he had sensations in his abdomen, stomach, chest, and throat.

If emotions can be thought of as colors, then a felt sense is a blend—often elusive, vague, temporary, subtle, and hard to describe. Some people feel too much; others too little:

When Harry felt flooded, focusing allowed him to acknowledge the sensations without feeling overwhelmed. He found that attending to the feeling lightened, softened, and relaxed it, and it often disappeared completely.

For the person who blocks feelings, this process allows them to tune in and listen to their body. As in any good listening, there are some important elements: a welcoming presence, holding the space, hearing the essence, and staying in present time.[9] There is a message that will come to your notice if you can establish an accepting, even trustful relationship to the feeling. In Ann Cornell's words, "when [the emotions] are allowed to be, they settle down and have a conversation with you."[10] It is like greeting a wild but friendly animal in a forest. Focusing is a way of tuning in to the wisdom of our bodies.

All this is important because some early experiences leave a memory in the body. It is such feelings and bodily sensations that carry the memory and provide a link to early preverbal learning.[11] While this can be distorted, it is still a valuable source of insight about early learning.[12]

We can, of course, "switch off" to the body. This has psychological labels such as "dissociation" or "depersonalization." Both are a desensitizing of the relationship to the body—quite the opposite of focusing as discussed here:

Martha just kept busy. She said, "I don't have time to feel anything. Not that I would want to since my children moved away."

The body is ever present. Its importance cannot be overemphasized, but it is hard to fully acknowledge its multidimensional character. Mindfulness and focusing have been mentioned as ways to increase our awareness of the body.

Reflect: In what ways does your body send you signals? For example, headaches or a stress rash might remind you that you are overworking and not taking self-care seriously. As a child, did you have any physical reactions to stresses in your home life?

THEOLOGICAL PERSPECTIVES

The body has had an uncertain place in the Christian tradition.[13] Unlike the Hebrews, with their earthy awareness of life, our theological perspective has been "seduced," if that is the right term, by Greek philosophers. Plato, for example, sharply contrasted the eternal value of the soul with the temporal "death bound" nature of the body.[14] The philosophy of Descartes led to the mind–body split and provided yet another way of devaluing the body. Perhaps we can agree that both devaluing the body and dividing the unity of the person are problematic.

The body has spiritual significance. A lot of Jesus's ministry was to the body: touching, healing, feeding. He mixed his own spit to heal the blind man (John 9:6). Paul opposed early dualistic thinking in the early church (1 Corinthians 6:15, 19–20). The biblical perspective on the body was essentially Hebraic, with a healthy appreciation of the body into which God breathed life (Genesis 2:7).[15] This is in contrast to the warped message that the body is "a hindrance to spiritual maturity, and, at worst, inherently evil or the ultimate source of sin."[16]

There are important theological themes that honor our physical selves. We are created as embodied creatures in the *imago dei* (the image of God; Genesis 1:27). The whole person (not the disembodied soul) is somehow necessary to bear the image of God and will ultimately share in eternal life. The Son of God became fully human in the incarnation (Philippians 2:6–8). On the third day, Jesus rose bodily from the dead (1 Corinthians 15:12–28, 35–49). A sophisticated somatology is provided by Ola Sigurdson in *Heavenly Bodies*.[17] This has implications for an integrative Christocentric spiritual formation.[18]

The body and its materiality have become a focus for theology.[19] Touch can convey relationality, and Graham Ward noted that touch is a reaching beyond the boundaries of oneself to find a place not yet given, a future not yet received.[20]

There are gender differences. Adam Cooper observed that sexual difference and affective reciprocity stand as a created sign pointing to the even greater fact that we are created for communion with God.[21] The various dimensions of human experience include the sensual and later the erotic, although this has been a point of denigration of the body.[22] It is possible to have a "holistic vision of the spiritual sense that does not elide the body, women and others in favor of the spirit but *re*-values the bodily and emotional aspects of *eros*."[23] This also reconciles difference and unity. It points to the divine–human relationship as well.[24]

It is obvious that we bring our body into our relationship with God.

CHURCH PRACTICE

The worship of the church, guided by liturgy, is experienced in the body. It is the place of God indwelling.[25] The church is the "Spirit-filled locus of the incarnate Lord's ongoing redemptive activity in history . . . a performative divine action."[26]

The practice of the church has often "got it right." Touch communicates connection with "passing the peace" or "holy hugs." There is also the touch of blessing, the laying on of hands with perhaps oil for healing, the imposition of ashes in Holy Week, and the sprinkling of holy water in the renewal of baptismal vows. Many Christians practice adult baptism, usually by total immersion. I am not arguing a theological point here, but simply noting a physical experience with the water.

Can we touch Christ? Well, it is possible symbolically. Last Sunday (as I write this) I held Christ. The minister in the Uniting Church where I worship had broken off a chunk of bread from a large loaf. It was dipped by an elder into the "wine" and the congregation held the elements to partake together:

> I held the bread with wine for about five minutes. I sensed the weight of Christ. My mind went to his sacrificial love and our participation in him:
>
> I experienced touch through ordination. It happened three times: when I was being ordained in the Christian and Missionary Alliance; when I was later dea-coned in the Anglican or Episcopal Church; and when I was ordained as a priest. Each time, I received the laying on of hands, which I felt as a weight of tradition and the support of my colleagues.

There can also be a sense of absence. Many Christians find significance in fasting. This is a discipline with physical implications. How do you respond when you are hungry or thirsty? What does the experience of hunger remind you of? Is Lent a time of giving up something?

We also experience the body through movement. Simple physical activity is part of life: walking, play, sport, games, and dancing. In church, participating in ritual usually involves movement. Sometimes we join in religious dramas, such as Palm Sunday processions. When I was the minister of Holy Covenant Anglican Church, I encouraged people at a Good Friday service to write something they regretted on a sheet of paper and then nail it to the cross at the front of the church. It was a powerful enactment of a spiritual reality in Christ. We can also think of the spiritual significance of being embraced. It is likely that this extends to feeling at peace in the cosmic order and ultimately some sense of connection with God.

Pilgrimage is important in many religious traditions, including the Christian one. It is usually associated with some understanding of a sacred place. When I was in ministry, I visited Jerusalem and many of the biblical sites in Israel and beyond, including Mount Sinai. Surprisingly, I found visiting the Wailing Wall the most intense of my experiences in the Holy Land. A number of my friends have walked the *Camino de Santiago* in Spain.

Reflect: Is there a place from your childhood that you think of as a sacred place? Can you go there? Stand in that place and feel the connection to your childhood. The first church I remember as a child was St. Aidan's in Narrabundah, Canberra, which is not far from where I now live.

Walking a labyrinth is a meditative experience. There is only one path to the center and out. Labyrinths are often found at retreat centers. People find it helpful to walk in a meditative way. Feel the sense of movement, your feet and your motion toward God. Think of the journey inward as toward God or Christ, then finding them in the center and then walking out as movement toward re-engaging with the world. There is a labyrinth where I work at the Australian Centre for Christianity and Culture. Google for directions to a local one.

One of the tasks of the church is to imagine God's presence in the world.[27] Both touch and movement are creative expressions of this.

WEEK 5 STUDY GROUP

Pastor Mike began the group with a question:

> What age are you before God? Before you rush to say your present age, think about it. Do you relate to God as a child, adolescent, young adult, adult, or aged person? If your imagined age is different from your chronological age, think about what that might mean. As you think back, did you miss a stage in your religious development?

This question was met with a shocked silence. For about a minute, no one said anything.

Stan broke the silence: "I've only been a Christian for five years. It was Cindy's example of life that spoke to me. I feel young—not a child but perhaps an adolescent—maybe 15 years old." Cindy said, "I feel as if I'm an adult believer, but I think I missed having a childlike faith. Something is definitely missing in my Christian development." There were other comments, but the group clearly got Mike's point about the age we feel before God.

Mike then had people share their photos. It was a show-and-tell with a lot of hilarity. Stan showed himself as a five-year-old standing outside the family home. When it was Kylie's turn, she brought out a photo of herself at age eleven attending a birthday party with school friends. Mike asked:

> Do you remember when your photo was taken? Do you look happy? Who else is in the photos? Who is beside you? Do you feel close to anyone in the picture? This might indicate attachment. Did you find a picture of yourself in a spiritual setting, such as being baptized?

He used this to explain how early spiritual experience can come through sight. Monica had a photo of herself standing in front of her childhood Lutheran Church. She said, "There was a wonderful stained-glass window, which I used to stare at in services. It spoke to me as a child. The picture was of Jesus being baptized." Len recalled being in a church with a verse written on the wall: "In large letters, 'Come unto me all ye that labor and are heavy laden, and I will give you rest' (Matthew 11:28). I can still see the words and I think it was in the King James Version." Mike said, "Yes, that sounds right."

Mike then lit a candle in the center of the group, "See the dance of the flame. Notice the light it gives off and the shadows created. What was the source of light in your childhood? Where were the shadows? Where did you hide?" He then introduced the steps of *visio divina*:

- Quieten your inner noise; put yourself in the presence of God.
- Look at the image with God's eyes and if possible register His delight.
- Notice what stirs within you. What responses, memories and feelings? Does it connect with your life?
- Respond to God from what you are feeling. How would you incorporate it into a prayer?[28]

Monica found this a profound experience: "Wow! It really took me into a sense of God's presence. I feel reverence, perhaps mystery and something beyond." She thought about her childhood: "It really wasn't that long ago. But I had a Christian family and church was part of our life. I think I had the sense of God quite often. I suppose I was fortunate; it was never hard for me to believe."

Mike then asked people to think about their tradition of worship. What shaped their understanding of God? He said that his earliest experience of worship was in the Presbyterian Church and asked:

Was yours traditional, liturgical, charismatic, contemporary, Pentecostal? Think about what you did with your body. When did you stand? Did you kneel? Pass the greeting of peace? Who touched you? How? Did you receive a blessing, say from a priest, while you were kneeling at the altar rail?

This resulted in some discussion about the importance of the touch. Mary said, with tears in her eyes, "Since John died last year, I miss the intimacy and touch we shared. It really helps when I get hugs in church."

The final topic of conversation was introduced by Mike: "Where do you sense God in your body? John Wesley described his conversion as 'I felt my heart strangely warmed.' Like Wesley, I sometimes feel God's presence in my chest." Len identified his stomach: "Bowels?" Stan commented, "I hear God's voice, so in my head." At times, Sally felt "warm all over, so my whole body."

Mike assigned a task for the coming week. He asked the members of the group to recall any other memories associated with the other senses: hearing, smell and taste. Everyone held hands for a final prayer.

SUMMARY

We have explored some of the ways we can learn through our physical selves. We notice both internal and external sensations. This can be intensified using the technique of focusing. All this has profound implications for early learning because the infant or young child can encounter transcendence in ways not limited by cognitive development. Over the centuries, there have been mixed responses to the body in the church and theological tradition. We can observe that the body is involved both in liturgy and church practice.

NOTES

1. Donald W. Winnicott, *The child, the family, and the outside world*, Penguin, Harmondsworth, 1964, 17, 44.

2. Paul Ricoeur, *Fallible man*, revised edition, trans. Charles A. Kelbley, Fordham University Press, New York, 1986, 9–10.

3. Klaus Wiegerling, "The superfluous body: Utopias of information and communication technology," in Regina Ammicht-Quinn and Elsa Tamez (eds), *The body and religion*, SCM Press, London, 2002, 20.

4. Colin McGinn, *Prehension: The hand and the emergence of humanity*, The MIT Press, Cambridge, Massachusetts, 2015.

5. Rothschild, *The body remembers*, 57.

6. Lecia Bushak, "Mindfulness vs meditation: The difference between these two pathways to well-being and peace of mind," *Medical Daily*, March 10, 2016, online: www.medicaldaily.com/mindfulness-meditation-differences-377346.

7. Jon Kabat-Zinn, *Wherever you go, there you are: Mindfulness meditation in everyday life*, Hyperion, New York, 1994, 4.

8. A good introduction is provided by Ann W. Cornell, *The power of focusing: A practical guide to emotional self-healing*, New Harbinger, Oakland, California, 1996.

9. Cornell, *The power of focusing*, 18.

10. Cornell, *The power of focusing*, 16.

11. We can assert this and yet be cautious about coming to simplistic conclusions. It is a complex picture. For example, Tristine Rainer asserted, "The body doesn't lie. If you can articulate the feelings in your body, present or past, you can generally reach your own complex truth." Quoted in Cepero, *Journaling as a spiritual practice*, 63.

12. Rothschild, *The body remembers*, xv.

13. Jean-Guy Nadeau, "Dichotomy or union of soul and body? The origins of the ambivalence of Christianity to the body," in Regina Ammicht-Quinn and Elsa Tamez (eds), *The body and religion,* Concilium 2, 2002, 57–65.

14. Conrado Eggers Lan, "Body and soul in Plato's anthropology," *Kernos*, 1995, 8:107–12.

15. Jewish thought was later influenced by Greek philosophy and dualism, but it was not the original biblical view; Louis Jacobs, "The body in Jewish worship: Three rituals examined," in Coakley, *Religion and the body*, 71–89, at 72.

16. Gregg R. Allison, "Towards a theology of human embodiment," *Southern Baptist Journal of Theology*, 2009, 13(2):5.

17. Sigurdson, *Heavenly bodies*.

18. Alexandria Blake Ford, "The implications of an evangelical theology of the body for Christocentric spiritual formation," *Proquest Dissertations*, EdD Thesis, 2018 (10816332), 1–136. There is also a study on Christian ideals relating to the body; Heather L. Jacobson, "Theology and the body: Sanctification and bodily experiences," *Psychology of Religion and Spirituality*, 2013, 5(1):41–50.

19. Mark Godin, "Touch and trembling: Intimating interdisciplinary bodies," in Heather Walton (ed.), *Literature and theology: New interdisciplinary spaces*, Routledge, New York, 2016, 155.

20. Graham Ward, *Christ and culture*, Blackwell, Malden, Massachusetts, 2005, 67.

21. Adam G. Cooper, *Holy Eros: A liturgical theology of the body*, Angelicopress, Kettering, Ohio, 2014, 2.

22. By an emphasis on virginity and celibacy; Andrew Louth, "The body in Western Catholic Christianity," in Coakley, *Religion and the body*, 111–30.

23. Michelle Voss Roberts, *Tastes of the divine: Hindu and Christian theologies of emotion*, Fordham University Press, New York, 2014, 104.

24. Sigurdson, *Heavenly bodies*, 489–90.

25. Cooper, *Holy Eros*, 6.

26. Cooper, *Holy Eros*, 7.

27. Sigurdson, *Heavenly bodies*, 7.

28. Calhoun, *Spiritual disciplines handbook*, 48.

Chapter Seven

Hearing

Life is full of sounds. There is beauty in birdsong and perhaps noise in the environment and the family circle, with siblings arguing, music playing and, possibly, the sound of a TV in the background. There is plenty of auditory input to consider. How do we deal with all this in early learning?

FROM BIRTH

Any sound will potentially get the attention of an infant. He will look in the direction of a voice, or toward the threat of a loud, sharp noise. [1] Singing can soothe. He enjoys creating sounds with a rattle.[2] This shows that from birth we are responsive to a range of sounds.

Even before a baby can understand words, a parent or carer will speak to him, communicating through tone of voice.[3] Parents are encouraged by experts to smile, talk, sing, and read to the growing baby. Many adults use a special voice, perhaps high pitched and with an exaggerated expression, possibly mimicking the female or nurturing voice. The natural "ba-ba" and "goo-goo" sounds from parents imitate and take seriously the sounds made by the baby. Babies answer back with their own "baby talk." There is delight when adults respond. And a baby is more likely to approach a new toy when he hears a positive tone from a parent.[4]

This is part of a larger "package" of communication that is reinforced by smiles, mirroring facial expressions, and gestures. In the first three months, the baby will respond to the voice, often getting excited and reacting with smiles, gurgles, and waving arms and legs. In the next few months, he will realize that his talk is important to the parent and look for a reaction. He will experiment with more sounds, raising and lowering the pitch of his voice. At about five months, he will heed a sharp warning of "No!"

Naming objects helps to develop language. Usually, by 8–12 months, the baby will say "mama" or "dada," although initially this may be accidental since words are more hit-or-miss. All this builds the foundation for later interpersonal skills.

Music is heard. It is a delight for both children and adults. Two of my grandchildren are now being encouraged to read music and play piano. Of course, their mother encourages them in regular practice, but the positive benefits are already obvious. Playing an instrument enables us to listen to music in a different way.

Reflect: What were the sounds of your childhood? Did you live in the country or city? This might have influenced you in different ways. I noticed, when living in Boston, there were often what sounded like gunshots (but may have been cars backfiring). What was the tone of your family life: peaceful, conflicted, frightening? How do you think such sounds shaped your early learning?

SACRED HEARING

We listen in a variety of ways. Religious stories have been told for millennia. I read Bible stories to our four children. Sacred music would often play in the background. Our children grew up attending church, where they heard the Bible read and everyone sang sacred songs. While they might not have always been attentive, I like to think that such experiences left a legacy. Adele Calhoun has commented, "The world is filled with reasons to be downcast. But deeper than sorrow thrums the unbroken pulse of God's joy, a joy that will yet have its eternal day."[5]

Sound has its origin in God because he spoke the world into being.[6] Many churches have made hearing the word central to the gathered community. The Bible is read aloud, a sermon is preached, and hearts are open to hearing God.

Think for a moment about the experience of being addressed. Someone wants to get our attention. A person talks to us, perhaps expecting a response. Many have found that God addresses the believer with a sense of his voice. Samuel, in the Old Testament, heard "Samuel. Samuel." He ran to Eli, thinking his master had called (1 Samuel 3:4). This happened three times before Eli realized that God had been calling him and that he should answer "Speak Lord for your servant is listening" (3:10). Samuel began his prophetic vocation by hearing the voice of God. We answer God's call in diverse ways to be incorporated into his larger story of redemption.[7]

We can listen to God in prayer. Many Christians have a sense that God communicates in this way. There are also creative techniques to encourage listening. I like the dialogue method of journaling. For example:

Robert thought of himself as a five-year-old sitting by a stream in a forest. Jesus came and sat beside him.

Jesus: How are you doing?

Robert: I like this place but I feel lonely. I don't have a brother or sister to play with.

Jesus: That's sad.

Robert: But I have you at the moment. It's nice to play games with a grown-up because Mom and Dad are too busy these days.

Jesus: What would you like to play?

Robert: Catching a baseball.

Jesus: That would be fun. Let's do it now.

Robert then thought about what he had learned as a young child but had since forgotten: "Then I knew it was possible to relate to Jesus or God in a natural childlike way. To play. I have since added so much to make good any relationship with God which feels artificial and, well, hard. I know what I have to get back to." He had understood how his body was overloaded with stress and that he had lost the ability to relax and play.

While the spoken word in church is essential, it is limiting if this is the only approved means of sacred communication. Some Protestant churches have judged the other senses to be associated with idolatry. In more liturgical services, the spoken word has an important place, but there are other senses God can use.

Many people love singing hymns or being in a church choir. Music is a way of sacred hearing. Who has not been moved by listening to Handel's *Messiah* or Bach's Mass in B minor? I have also enjoyed popular gospel songs, including Hillsong's *Oceans*. I know that my life would be impoverished without sacred music.

Reflect: What was the place of music for you as a child? Go back as far as you can remember. Can you imagine the mood of your family through what music was played? Was there any gospel or sacred music?

SUMMARY

There is no need to emphasize the importance of hearing. We have thought about the way parents talk to infants and why that is important. Listening is also the means by which we are mostly taught, so words are the source of much of what we now believe to be true. This includes both ordinary and spiritual knowing. The church for most people is a place of communal listening. It is important to highlight the importance of this mechanism for early learning.

NOTES

1. Bower, *The rational infant*, 12.
2. Bower, *The rational infant*, 75.
3. There is research that indicates that very young infants prefer their native language; Christine Moon, Robin P. Cooper, and William P. Fifer, "Two-day-olds prefer their native language," *Infant Behavior and Development*, 1993, 16:495–500.
4. Sarah Gerson, Meridith Gattis, and Netta Weinstein, "Before babies understand words they understand tones of voice," *The Conversation*, August 24, 2017.
5. Calhoun, *Spiritual disciplines handbook*, 29.
6. Stephen H. Webb, *The divine voice: Christian proclamation and the theology of sound*, Brazos Press, Grand Rapids, Michigan, 2004, 14.
7. Cooper, *Holy Eros*, 72.

Chapter Eight

Smell

Odor is universal. Almost everything has a smell. My sense of smell is limited, but when I walked my dog I delighted in that creature's interaction with the world through its cold attentive nose. What might we learn through our sense of smell?

GROWING UP

Odor is also part of the world that welcomes the newborn infant. This includes the smell of her mother, her milk, other food, and household smells. Perhaps an open fire. Smells associated with family life carry a sense of belonging and, ideally, being safe and secure. This is equally true for us as adults. This can be manipulated—hence the oft-cited real estate advice to cook a cake or brew some coffee before a home inspection.

A New Zealander friend had vivid childhood memories associated with:

> . . . the smell of roast lamb on a Sunday afternoon or the damp bush where we used to make huts. Passionfruit from the vine outside or the smell of Dad's aftershave. The smell of sea and salty air, the smell of the school classroom and the 30 kids at the end of physical education.

There is a complex interaction of the senses of smell and taste. It is not widely appreciated that we can *smell* through our mouths when eating, since volatile chemicals rise up through the nasopharynx. Hence, smell is a dual modality in that it explores objects both through the external world and within the body.[1] There is also texture involved (e.g., when eating pork crackling).

Smell helps us navigate the world. It also provides an early warning system alerting us to fire, toxic fumes, and polluted environments. We justly hesitate or refuse to eat something that does not smell right.

Reflect: What smells do you associate with your childhood? I think of disinfectant. My mother maintained hospital-level cleanliness, despite the efforts of her two sons.

SACRED SMELL

Christianity emerged in a world in which smell mattered:

> [S]mells revealed things about the object, person, or place from which they wafted . . . they were invisible, because they were transitory, because they were mobile, because they lingered, because of their potency to change substance or experience or meaning.[2]

Hence, pleasant smells were associated with the good; odors could cleanse, purify, ward off, or heal; they could contaminate, pollute, endanger.[3] This sense was used for discernment, as a way of knowing. Smell was a singularly effective means of discerning divine presence or absence, demonic activity, or moral condition.[4]

Smell has always been important in worship. Incense was used in the worship of the Old Testament (Psalms 141:2).[5] Perfumed oil is cited in the New Testament; for example, in the accounts of the sinful woman washing the feet of Jesus, of Mary of Bethany and of Jesus's burial). There was an ancient custom of using oil to show respect. Sick individuals were anointed for healing (James 5:14–15). In the apostolic tradition, oil was blessed immediately after the Eucharist, and that was in common practice before the fourth century. Incense was associated with sacrifice (e.g., of the early martyrs), and it represented the human initiative toward God. The human–divine encounter was marked by a sweet fragrance.

When Christianity became "official," incense was used in public processions. Emperor Constantine gave censers to the church in Rome. By the fifth century, incense was common in the Christian liturgy.[6] The newly established church placed increasing emphasis on claiming the physical world as a realm of positive spiritual encounters through engagement with physical experience. This period introduced pilgrimage, relics, cults of saints, church art and architecture, the enrichment of liturgy with the grandeur of imperial court ceremony, and temple imagery. Incense and perfumed holy oils "continued the trajectory with the teaching that in the incarnation the divine itself had entered into matter, sanctifying and renewing the whole of material existence."[7]

This acceptance signaled a shift in attitude. Earlier writers condemned incense, but now it drenched every form of Christian ceremonial, and scented oils gained sacramental usage in sanctuary lamps. There were other smells, such as freshly baked bread for the Eucharist. Susan Harvey has noted that the experience of worship was a "ritually fashioned experience."[8]

Does it make sense to talk about sacred smells? What about the presence of flowers in church? The smells of incense or rose petals and rosewater are used for Hindu worship. Such smells can be distinctive and an invitation to worship. Christians inhabited the world with a sense of transcendence. Olfactory experience could mirror sacramental reality: to smell God was to know God as a transcendent and transforming presence (actively known through bodily experience).[9]

SUMMARY

The sense of smell is essential. It is a means of discernment. It was important in the culture of the early church. Incense and oils were used in worship. Smell has always been about things unseen, and it reminds us that invisible realities such as God should be noticed. Smell is another pathway for early learning.

NOTES

1. Auvray & Spence, "Multisensory perception of flavor," 1022.
2. Susan A. Harvey, *Scenting salvation: Ancient Christianity and the olfactory imagination*, University of California Press, Berkeley, California, 2006, 1.
3. Harvey, *Scenting salvation*, 2.
4. Harvey, *Scenting salvation*, 100.
5. There were also smells associated with sacrifice (Genesis 8:20–9:1).
6. Harvey, *Scenting salvation*, 75.
7. Harvey, *Scenting salvation*, 59.
8. Harvey, *Scenting salvation*, 57.
9. Harvey, *Scenting salvation*, 65.

Chapter Nine

Taste

Food is the stuff of life. Everything living eats in one way or another. The sense associated with food is taste, but even something not edible, such as dirt, has a taste. So taste is also a significant guide and useful for discernment. In this chapter, we will explore the place of this sense in early learning.

FROM BIRTH

Taste, naturally, is present at birth. The baby drinks milk—maternal or bottled. This extends later to eating solids and eventually to a whole range of tastes, from bland to highly spiced.

There is something immediate about taste. We can see a storm in the distance, hear thunder, and maybe smell the change in the atmosphere, but we can touch or taste only something that is present.[1] Taste is the sense that encounters the abundance of creation in food. It is intimate, bringing food to our lips, mouth and body, then ingesting and incorporating it into our flesh, tendons, blood, and bones.[2] And eating does not end with taste. There is a tearing apart, chewing, devouring, consuming, and incorporating of food. Indeed, food matters. It shows a "complex interaction between self and other; object and subject; appetite and digestion; aesthetics, ethics and politics; nature and culture; and creation and divinity."[3]

There is the potential to create community through food. The wonderful film *Babette's Feast* (1987) illustrated this. Directed by Gabriel Axel, it was based on a story written by Isak Dinesen. It was set in a remote impoverished coastal village, to which Babette flees from revolutionary Paris. For fourteen years, she cooked basic fare for two sisters. Then Babette won a lottery, which funded the creation of a real French dinner for the sisters and a small congregation. This was to honor the deceased founding pastor's 100th birthday. Gradually, it emerged that Babette was a famous chef of the Café Anglais of Paris. The dinner for twelve came at a cost of 10,000 francs. One of the sisters, Martine, said tearfully, "Now you will be poor the rest of your life." Babette answered, "An artist is never poor." The other sister, Philippa, added, "But this is not the end, Babette. In paradise you will be the great artist God meant you to be." The feast led to a renewed community.

I remember bland food in my childhood. My father must have once complimented my mother on her meat loaf, for we had it once a week for as long as I can remember. Mercifully, Australia is now multicultural and there are literally dozens of ethnic restaurants within walking distance of where I live. I have found exploring different tastes a joy in my adult years. I enjoy fine dining on special occasions. It is a delight.

Reflect: There are many attitudes associated with eating in the family. Was it used for emotional comfort? A guilty pleasure? Or were you fearful because of the risk of becoming overweight? Could it be simply the pleasure of everyone getting together, enjoying one another's company with food as the excuse? Can you articulate your early learning in relation to food?

SACRAMENTAL FOOD

In the Old Testament, divine law guided the activities of daily life. This included what was eaten. The book of Genesis distinguished between allowed and forbidden food. Adam and Eve were not to eat the fruit of the tree of the knowledge of good and evil (Genesis 2:16–17). Notice that the appeal of the serpent to Eve included the senses: "When you eat of it your eyes will be opened, and you will be like God, knowing good and evil." (Genesis 3:5). Eve saw, she touched, and she tasted. The transgression led to the expulsion of the first couple from the Garden of Eden. The serpent was also cursed: "dust you shall eat all the days of your life" (Genesis 3:14). The fall is a false vision that separates humanity from God.[4] But the principle of how to live in harmony with God's will was established.

Also in the Old Testament, God provided manna in the wilderness: "It was like coriander seed, white and the taste of it was like wafers made with honey" (Exodus 16:31). This was a sign of God's commitment to nourish the people, whom He had promised to settle in a land that flows with milk and honey (Exodus 3:8).

An elaborate system of offerings and sacrifices is described in the Old Testament. Some sacrifices were completely burned to provide a pleasing aroma to God (see, for example, Leviticus 1:9). There were feast days and festivals on which the people of God could participate in eating the sacrificed animals. There were prohibitions, and some food was reserved for the priestly caste; for example, the priests ate unleavened cakes made from the grain offering (Leviticus 6:16–17).[5] The people could eat of the sacrificed animal in the peace offering (Leviticus 3:1–2, 7:11–21). Food has a link to sacrifice and death, and also to intimate relationships. It is seen as a gift from God and part of participation in the divine life: "O, taste and see that the Lord is good" (Psalms 34:8).

Taste is the means of savoring food. It is a way of knowing. This is illustrated by the relation between *sapere* (to taste) and *sapiens* (being wise) in Latin.[6] Taste is associated with intellectual, ethical, and aesthetic discernment.[7] Taste as a sense is the medium and guide to the soul, intensified to be an intense mystical experience: "to know God is to savor God."[8]

Taste points to the *relationality* of food. Roland Barthes argued that food is a system of communication.[9] This is seen in the tea ceremony in Japanese culture. This has theological significance when it points to the "in-betweenness of the divine–human relationality."[10]

The profound significance of the Eucharist is honored in almost every Christian tradition. This expresses the truth that:

> our food-ways could be seen as a narrative performance of how societies construct notions of self and community, and how their relationship with the world; and these may also include a belief in spiritual, invisible, and transcendent entities or realities.[11]

Through taste, it is intensified to become a mystical experience of union with God. There is a sense that humanity ate to become separated from God and eats to reunite in the Eucharist—the bread of life. There is a relationality of being.[12] The Eucharist is a Trinitarian gesture of hospitality so that God becomes food and drink, so that God can become part of the partaker's body, and, even more, so that humanity can become part of God's own body.[13] It is a way of knowing God, who gives the divine self in the Eucharist. Sin is the refusal of God's love as nourishment. There is knowledge through taste—participation—and this conflicts with the Cartesian division of body and mind. The result is more than information. Knowledge, according to theologian Graham Ward, is always interactive.[14]

WEEK 6 STUDY GROUP

Pastor Mike began the group with a mindfulness meditation: "Pause and listen. Can you identify five different sounds? I can hear air-conditioning, a door shutting in the house, footsteps, my clothes rustling, and birdsong." Other group members heard different sounds, including a car driving past, the rustle of trees, and wind.

He then asked each person to use their notebook to record a dialogue:

Can you imagine yourself at about age 5 or 6? Place your child-self in a church or sacred space that's meaningful for you. This may be in nature. Write a dialogue with your child-self, perhaps asking such things as:

- Are you happy?
- Who would you like to be with you?
- Is there anything you like doing in church?
- What have you learned about God?
- What might you have learned about spiritual reality that you, as an adult, have since forgotten?
- How do you like to play?

Some of the group had difficulty with this exercise, but all persisted. Sally was totally engaged in her dialogue with her inner child:

I think that there's a lot about my childhood belief in God that I've forgotten. I think that taking philosophy classes has made me more skeptical. It's removed some of the magic I had as a child, in which everything was sacred. I've lost a lot to be a "rational" adult.

A number were surprised when their dialogue with early self "took off," with a result that was surprising. Cindy brought Jesus into the conversation, which became "three-way."

Mike introduced the sense of taste with a mindfulness exercise. He handed out a raisin to each in the group. He led them in a series of awareness steps:

Look at the raisin, the wrinkles and how the light plays on it. Feel the weight of it in your hand. Lift it to your nose. Can you smell it? Then bite into half the raisin and focus on the taste in your mouth. See how it fills your mouth with a distinctive taste. Slowly chew it and notice the grittiness. Feel how you respond with saliva. And, when you're finished with the first bite, put the rest of the raisin in your mouth. Try to chew it even more slowly and notice the flavor.

The members of group were astonished at how this exercise focused them on an everyday taste. Kylie said, "I usually just grab a handful of raisins to snack on. I put small boxes in the lunch box for my children. Now that I think about it, I rarely taste anything."

There was talk of tastes remembered from childhood. Mary recalled church fellowship meals: "There were often new tastes. My mother was a very bland cook . . . pretty much boiled meat and potatoes for us. It was a new experience. And then an Indian family joined our church. Their curries were amazing."

Stan remembered having a Seder service and meal at his previous church. Seder is the traditional Jewish celebration of the Exodus:

> The church gathered for a family meal with a candle and liturgy. A Seder plate was prepared with five foods: shank bone (*zeroa*), egg (*beitzah*), bitter herbs (*maror*), a vegetable (*karpas*) and a sweet paste (*haroset*). All this represents the bitterness of slavery.

Mike recalled the four traditional questions, asked by the youngest child: Why is this night different from all other nights? Why do we eat these special foods and sit in this way? One version ends with the question: How does this journey to freedom continue? What does it mean to so taste the setbacks or disappointments of life?" There was some enthusiasm to do this as part of the preparation for Easter in the following year.

Mike did a final exercise for the sense of smell. He lit a stick of incense and said:

> Mindfully focus on this smell. What associations do you have? What memories come back? How does it feel? Allow your mind to drift to other smells, perhaps from childhood, such as perfume, a walk in a forest after it's rained, the salt of the sea as you walk along a beach.

Mike asked the group to find fifteen minutes during the week ahead to be silent before God: "I will be interested in any feedback from the experience of silence."

SUMMARY

We do not need to be reminded of the importance of food. It is a matter of life and death for everything living. It is natural that we learn through the sense of taste, and this provides important early learning for the infant and growing child. It is one of the ways we relate to others. Food can create community, as illustrated by *Babette's Feast*. I have discussed manna in the wilderness and Old Testament rules about food. There is a sacred dimension to food that is seen in different ways in various religious traditions, but sacramentally in the Christian tradition.

We have explored early learning through the five senses. The task now shifts to trying to discover a message. This is the content of unconscious spiritual learning, which can be expressed in language. This provides new opportunities: "Aha! That is what I've learned." Content can be tested and challenged with a different perspective, which may come through understanding the experience and its unformulated message.

Sathianathan Clarke, Professor of Systematic Theology at Wesley Theological Seminary, Washington, D.C., told of his childhood growing up with his father, who was a bishop in the Church of South India. He was loved unconditionally as a child and felt an inherent sense of goodness about himself. This was in contrast to the message of his church, which was that everyone is fallen and a sinner before God. He said, "My consistent childhood experience came in conflict with the theological narrative of the church, which was also preached by my father, an Evangelical preacher." He came to realize that his first understanding was positive and only later was the message of the church a secondary, generally negative, overlay giving him a different view of who he was. It was important for Sathi to sort out the conflicting messages.

Generally, it is a similar challenge for all of us to retain the positive or to counterbalance the negative. It is to this we now turn.

NOTES

1. Ryan, *Taste*, 39.

2. Angel F. Mendez-Montoya, *The theology of food: Eating and the Eucharist*, Wiley-Blackwell, Malden, Massachusetts, 2012, 1.

3. Mendez-Montoya, *The theology of food*, ix .

4. Mendez-Montoya, *The theology of food*, 84.

5. For a comprehensive treatment of the Old Testament rituals, see Roy E. Gane, *Cult and character: Purification offerings, Day of Atonement and theodicy*, Eisenbrauns, Winona Lake, Indiana, 2005.

6. Mendez-Montoya, *The theology of food*, 46.

7. Mendez-Montoya, *The theology of food*, 62.

8. Mendez-Montoya, *The theology of food*, 70.

9. Roland Barthes, "Towards a psychosociology of contemporary food consumption," in Carole Counihan and Penny Van Esterik (eds), *Food and culture: A reader*, 2nd edition, Routledge, New York, 2008, 21.

10. Mendez-Montoya, *The theology of food*, 37.

11. Mendez-Montoya, *The theology of food*, 6.

12. Mendez-Montoya, *The theology of food*, 110.

13. Mendez-Montoya, *The theology of food*, 109.

14. Graham Ward, *Christ and culture*, Blackwell, Oxford, U.K., 2005, 95.

Chapter Ten

Revisiting Infantile Experience

William Robinson is a leading Australian artist. He has a unique vision of the rain forests of southern Queensland. Many of his paintings, such as *Twin Pools,* draw the viewer into the complex interdependence of the vegetation with ferns, climbing creepers, and native grasses. Trees reach out with branches at odd angles. There are multiple perspectives, somewhat like those in a Cubist painting. There is a sense of time passing, and of dawn, day and night across the work. In one of his characteristic images, stars are reflected in the pools.

Infantile experience can also be seen from various vantage points. We have explored this, for example, with the five senses. We will now consider whether there is a preferred sense and look at two other possible influences on spiritual development.

LOVE LANGUAGE FOR GOD?

The five senses are important for both psychological and spiritual development. Have you identified your primary sense? This will tend to be what you most rely on. Maybe you have a secondary sense. It makes sense that this will apply equally to the spiritual realm. Have you noticed whether this is your preferred sense for communicating with God? Perhaps with this recognition we can relate more naturally to God and not "try on ill-fitting clothes" for our spiritual life:

Margaret did a Camino pilgrimage, walking a route from Portugal into Spain. The mode of walking made her feel as if she were both making a journey and becoming a new person. Pushing herself physically seemed important. At the end, when she arrived at the Cathedral of St. James, she said, "I have discovered God anew. It's wonderful."

My primary way of experiencing God is visual, through an appreciation of beauty. I am fortunate to live near the Australian National Gallery, which has a great collection of abstract expressionist art. Jackson Pollock's *Blue Poles*, with its intricate patterns of drip painting, is in the collection. Pollack, for me, echoes the creativity of God.

It is only natural to have a preferred sense for God. The popular author Gary Chapman suggested that there are *Five Love Languages*.[1] They do not directly parallel the five senses, but include receiving gifts, spending high-quality time, words of affirmation, acts of service, and physical touch. Chapman notes that we feel loved in different ways. This relates to our style of communication, which has a potential application to how we feel most comfortable relating to God.

Reflect: What do you consider to be your primary sense with God? Which exercises did you find most useful? Can you build on this in a creative way? For example, Manuel saw that touch was very important to him. He had a weekly massage and decided that he would visualize God touching him at this time: "After all, Jesus washed the feet of his disciples" (John 13:3–10).

ATTACHMENT OBJECTS

There are other perspectives on the early life of the infant and young child. One idea is that of a "transitional object." The psychoanalyst Donald Winnicott used this opaque term to refer to a child's early attachment to a teddy bear, blanket, soft toy, or some other object.[2] The reality of such childhood attachments is apparent to most parents. While I will continue to use Winnicott's term, I prefer the term "attachment object" because it is more indicative of the relationship between object and child:

> I remember that my daughter Kym had a jumpsuit made of terry cloth when she was a baby. She became too big for the suit, but kept wearing it to the point of disintegration. We visited Disneyland when she was about three and we bought her a soft pink terry-cloth mouse with big ears. Kym attached to the mouse but in time it, too, perished. This attachment was important for the first three or four years of her life, until she, like other children, simply grew out of it.

It is because of the gradual loss of interest in such things that they are called "transitional," though Sebastian, in the novel *Brideshead Revisited,* took his teddy bear Aloysius off to Oxford.[3]

Sometimes, we can see the links between breast–thumb–object. This was obvious with Kym. While breast-feeding, she used to finger her mother's terry-cloth robe. This transferred to her scratching at the cuff of her jumpsuit, while sucking her thumb, which continued to the terry-cloth mouse a couple of years later.

There is an important psychological process here. Initially, the baby is comforted, held, and fed by her mother. This is a blissful state of union that is obvious even to fathers, but the infant must eventually be detached from the mother and put in a cot to sleep. I am talking about the mother, but the process is potentially the same with any primary attachment figure, such as the father or another carer. The object is a reminder of the carer's soothing presence. In the example I have given, the texture evoked soothing in the absence of Jenny, Kym's mother. It was also the first "not-me" possession of the child.

This in-between psychological space is important, as Winnicott observed. He identified a transition to the internalization of the mother in the child's developing psyche. When this happens, the child is better able to self-soothe. This is an always available memory of the mother because it is part of the psyche. After internalization, there is no need for the original attachment object, so it is transitional and ultimately left behind.

We can identify three basic steps:

- the physical presence of the mother
- the symbolic reminder of mother
- the internalization of the mother, with the result that the object is no longer needed.

Winnicott drew attention to the early symbolic quality and to the "intermediate area of experiencing to which inner reality and external life both contribute."[4] This allows the child to take the holding function of parents, transfer it to the object, and pretend that it is under control. This assists the internalizing process, helps self-regulation, and eventually leads to a cohesive sense of self. This process is described in some detail by the analyst Marion Tolpin.[5]

Perhaps something similar happens with some older children who have an imaginary companion. This invisible friend may help in learning to relate to others. He or she may serve as a playmate or as a scapegoat for bad impulses. This, too, is like a transitional object and will disappear when there is no longer a need for it.

AND GOD

Winnicott believed that the blend of fantasy and reality becomes the basis for play, art, imagination, creativity, and religious experience. This is an interesting hypothesis, and I think it does point to the creative space where imagination flourishes in the psyche. The psychoanalyst Ana-Maria Rizzuto thought that God functions as a transitional object:

> [L]ike jugglers we sometimes call in our God and toss him around, sometimes we discard him because he is too colorless for our needs or too hot for us to handle. Some of us never get him out of the magician's box where we have placed him in childhood; others never stop throwing him around.[6]

But, arguably, God is not an object, and for most believers is God not transitional. Language tends to break down in this regard. However, this creative space appears to be relevant for psychological and religious development. Perhaps there is also a role for this early imagining of God in gaining leverage with oneself, with others, and with life in general. The point is that in this early stage the child is at least partially creating his or her God in the service of personal needs.

I have maintained throughout this book that our understanding of God is richly developed before any input from Sunday school. It is a complex, dynamic process in which the inner and outer worlds contribute:

> [T]he fantasy of the child certainly adds color, drama, glamour, and horror to the insignificant moments as well as to the real tragedies of everyday life. It is out of this matrix of facts, fantasies, wishes, hopes and fears, and in the exchanges with those incredible beings called parents, that the image of God is concocted.[7]

The psychoanalytic authors have been right to assert the role of fantasy. This realm will be inhabited by many figures in addition to parents: comical characters, movie heroes, witches, ogres, giants, space monsters, ghosts, devils, fairy-story figures . . . the list is endless. So, too, are our earliest imaginings of God filled with fantasy. Rizzuto elaborated:

> [T]ogether with this colorful crowd of characters and amidst intense anal, phallic, vaginal pre-occupations, fantasies, wishes and fears, God arrives. At first he may seem one more in the procession. Soon, however, he acquires a special superior status.[8]

The family may speak of Santa Claus, but it is done lightly, with a twinkle in the eye. But God deserves respect. In church, the house of God, the child is solemnly warned to sit still and be quiet! The little child is nevertheless bursting with theological interest: "Can you see angels? Does God have a wee-wee? Who made God?" Imagination may be almost unlimited, but equally the newborn has a good appreciation of reality. Both fantasy and reality must be held in tension.

The child gradually clarifies the distinction between God and his parents. Partly, this relates to the discovery that Mom and Dad are human and not omnipotent. Parents, for example, have parents. William Meissner has argued that the child will salvage some of his misplaced idealism by projecting it to an all-powerful and perfect God (who does not have parents!). The God images eventually become less mythical and fantastic: "[A]bout the age of five the representations of God, the parents and the child himself become more pedestrian."[9]

INFANTILE WILL

When might an infant or young child begin to express her will? We have seen that Daniel Stern identified a sense of agency as one of the infant's early precognitive capacities.[10] It is clear from observations of infants that there are many willful behaviors from birth. The infant is interested in people, examines objects, will follow them with her eyes, will cry when hungry, will laugh when amused, and will move and bring her hands together. A month or two later, she will recognize her mother's voice, and at about five months a stronger attachment will begin to form. She will roll over, sit up, put her fingers in her mouth, be interested in what her parent is eating, and reach for and grab anything nearby.

Every mother knows that her young child will assert independence. Perhaps this begins with gaze aversion at about four months, develops with gestures and vocal intonation at seven months, and shows as running away at fourteen months and as language ("No!") at about two years.[11]

An infant is born with awareness, an immediate capacity to learn, and a capacity to exercise agency. Yes, the context is one of dependence on carers, but agency is present, and that has many implications. A healthy child will develop self-esteem, identity, and well-being. These are the first steps on this important path. There are spiritual implications as the child gains confidence, learns to explore, to express ideas, to question and to come to her own beliefs.[12]

What is the infant's first learning in relation to agency? I think it might be about "getting Mom's attention." She will learn what works: smiling, gurgling, waving her arms, deliberately dropping things, and many other actions. Once her carer is looking, good things follow, such as food, a change of diaper, or being cuddled and held. Do you have any memories of trying to get an adult's attention? In this context, we can begin to think how we might first try to get God's attention.

I will raise an important, possibly speculative, line of thought that comes out of these considerations: we make early life choices. Some choices are so early that we have no memory of ever writing a life script.

I think about this in terms of my clinical experience, I have treated a number of patients who met the criteria for antisocial personality disorder, a severe form of which is found in the psychopath. It seems to me that psychopathy derives in part from an early life choice, probably before language, of "I'm going to get you before you get me." This is, of course, a survival tactic that can make sense in a home with little nurture and negative experiences of violence and abuse. As a life script, this choice is almost impossible to reverse. This has led me to wonder whether we all make life choices from an early age that carry through life.

This may be something that shapes our personality. Think of a person who is unassertive. The script is one of avoiding conflict: "I'll say yes to anything." Or to depend on others: "You're strong, and I'll rely on you for everything I need." A grandiose person has decided, "I'm superior to you and everyone else."

I think such decisions are part of the formation of personality and highly influential on later life choices. A similar theme was developed in transactional analysis with the idea of "script decisions."[13]

Does this apply in the spiritual realm? Probably.

Think about when a young child begins to grasp a notion of God. Perhaps it is not long before an attitude toward God is formed. There are many possible early reactions to the idea of God:

- God is scary. I need to keep away.
- God welcomes me and hugs me like my mother does.
- God watches and judges me.
- God will smack me when I do the wrong thing.
- God is always there.

It seems likely to me that such early perceptions of God lead to early spiritual choices. This sets the context for later belief or unbelief; acceptance or rejection; a walk toward God or a walk away.

This is a new area of my thinking but I suspect that infantile choice is important for, even formative of, later attitudes. This seems likely in both psychological development and spiritual formation.

Reflect: Is it possible that early decisions in relation to God are relevant to evangelism? How might the church think about the gospel message in light of this understanding? At what age do you think it is possible for an infant or young child to respond to a sense of God? Or even to choose to be a follower?

SUMMARY

We have seen that infants and children learn in diverse ways. This occurs through the senses. But we can go further with the assistance of Winnicott and Rizzuto. For many, maybe most, children, there is attachment to a special object that represents caretaking and provides soothing. This in-between state is a place for the mixing of reality and fantasy. It has been argued that this provides an important "space" for experiencing God. I have also raised the idea of infantile will and how it might influence later spiritual choices.

NOTES

1. Gary Chapman, *The five love languages: How to express heartfelt commitment to your mate*, Northfield Publishing, Chicago, Illinois, 1995.

2. Winnicott, *Playing and reality*, 1–34.

3. Evelyn Waugh, *Brideshead revisited*, Penguin, London, 1951.

4. Winnicott, *Playing and reality*, 2.

5. Marion Toplin, "On the beginnings of the cohesive self: An application of the concept of transmuting internalization to the study of the transitional object and signal anxiety," *The Psychoanalytic Study of the Child*, 1971, 26:316–52.

6. Rizzuto, *Birth of the living God*, 180. Sperry argues that God functions as a transitional phenomenon that allows a person to experience the other; Len Sperry, "From teddy bear to God image: Object relations theory and religious development," *Psychologists Interested in Religious Issues Newsletter*, Spring 1989, 14(2):5–8.

7. Rizzuto, *Birth of the living God*, 7.

8. Rizzuto, *Birth of the living God*, 193–94.

9. Rizzuto, *Birth of the living God*, 199.

10. Stern, *Interpersonal world*, 7.

11. Stern, *Interpersonal world*, 22.

12. Anonymous, "Promoting independence and agency," *Newsletter of the National Quality Standard Professional Learning Program*, 2013, 64:1–4.

13. See Claire Newton, *Transactional analysis—Part III (The scripts we follow)*, online: www.clairenewton.co.za/my-articles/transactional-analysis-part-iii-the-scripts-we-follow.html.

Chapter Eleven

Into Language

Our ability to express experience in language is central to realizing what has—paradoxically—been learned without language. It is a path that reveals early learning. And it also offers a way to change dysfunctional early learning, including spiritual beliefs.

WORDS ARE SECONDARY

Experience leads to language. This is a familiar process. I see a dramatic sunset. My reaction is "Wow!" Step 1: Experience. Step 2: Language. This happens via the five pathways of the senses: "It smells awful," "That's a bitter taste," or "I feel shivers down my back." None is initially verbal, with the exception of hearing words.

Consider an emotional reaction:

> *Nicole* had a stressful work evaluation with her supervisor. Later, she rang a friend to debrief. Her friend asked, "Well, how do you feel?" Nicole thought for a moment and said, "I have mixed feelings. Certainly, relief that it's over. Some disappointment. I expected more credit for the large project I did last year. But I was pleased that my supervisor said she would support me in getting a promotion. And there was a small raise in my salary."

This illustrates a normal process: experience, thought, then an attempt to put it into words and finally to gain understanding. Language facilitates insight. It is the same with spiritual experience. We have experiences that are potentially formative; sometimes they remain largely unconscious and are not put into words, but they shape our behavior:

When *Gary* was in high school, he lost his best friend in a hunting accident. The friend accidentally fired his gun while crossing a fence. Gary more or less buried the memory and froze his grief. Then he stopped attending the youth group at church. Decades later, he was able to put it into words: "I was mad at God. Why did God fail to protect my friend? He'd done nothing wrong!"

You might question Gary's conclusion, or you might agree based on experiences you have had. It seems that we often form beliefs that are not put into words or carefully considered. The first step is to revisit the original, largely unconscious, assumptions.

We have seen the importance of the five senses. They provide clues as to what was experienced, processed, and, potentially, learned. For example, a distinct smell might be a starting point. The original experience is revived and then expressed in language, which leads to a variety of options. Once a discovery can be articulated, it can be tested and disputed if necessary. Language matters in a secondary sense:

> *Sandra* remembered church potluck dinners. Her family was not well off, and others would bring ice cream: "That was the only time I would get to be like other kids and enjoy ice cream. I felt like I belonged in a big family, the church, and that God welcomed me there. I've always believed, and church is an important part of my life.

Our original learning was on a range from unconscious to conscious. If it was largely unconscious, then the discovery of spiritual learning may be surprising—not always, but generally producing an "Aha!" or surprising moment. It can be so strong that it is like being ambushed. Gradually, it dawns on us that this early learning wants to speak. There is a message to be heard. We have only to provide the opportunity. This can be done through the technique of sentence completion. This tool is so important that I will focus on it here.

SENTENCE COMPLETION

Sentence completion is one of the most effective ways to discover inarticulate learning. Ecker wrote about "naming into awareness."[1] Sentence completion is illustrated in the following account:

> *Barbara* wondered why she felt so unworthy when she received the Eucharist in her Roman Catholic church. She talked to the priest in a counseling session. He suggested: "Try this. Complete the sentence 'I am bad because . . .' Think about this and we can talk tomorrow."

Barbara was surprised by the answer: "I'm bad because I have freckles." She recalled her experience of being teased and shamed as a child because she had red hair and freckles. She judged herself as not just different but ugly and wanted to hide. At the core of herself, she concluded that she was bad. This is an example of dysfunctional learning that affected her sense of worthiness before God—which attending worship brought back to her.

To do: Try for yourself the following stem: "The most important thing I learned as a child was . . ."

A friend did this and ended the sentence with "you're on your own, kid!" This message revealed his implicit learning, providing a script of self-sufficiency throughout his life.

I tried this sentence completion:

I was surprised by my ending: "it's hard to be noticed." I recalled that my parents were emotionally entangled. While my basic needs were met, there was not a lot of noticing of me. This message explained my narcissistic quest (to be noticed). I can now see that was the basis of my implicit learning, which shaped my adult life. It is something I now accept as a mixed blessing, since it has driven me to some success, which I now enjoy.

Reflect: You might like to try any of the following sentence completions:

- As a child I learned that I must . . .
- I always accepted that I have to . . . with people I love.
- If I do something different, then the result will be . . .
- What I never question about myself is . . .

Try writing out four or five different completions. Then look over the list. Do any feel emotionally charged? This is a signal that your response is likely to contain hidden learning. Then refine the sentence until every word feels 100 percent right.

If nothing comes, then shift to another sensory pathway. For example, a visual image or a sound or a sense of touch may come. Stay with that sensation and see where it leads you. Then try to express what you feel in words.

When you have a statement that feels absolutely true, write it on a card and look at it once a day. Do nothing else in relation to the sentence for a week, or maybe two weeks. You might find that you are starting to question what you have written. Does another perspective arise? Do you start to question what you initially felt so certain about? You are in a process to challenge your hidden learning.

Also attempt this with early precognitive decisions you might have made:

- My most important decision as a child was to . . .
- One commitment I never question is . . .
- I've always known that I must . . .

When you first try the sentence completion exercise, you may encounter a wall of resistance. This is a good indication that something is present outside your awareness. It is as if you are in a boat and hit something in the water, unseen, that blocks your way. It is time to acknowledge and explore that. Resistance to completing a sentence is *significant* because it will be based on prior learning. Persist. Trial and error is fine, since it allows for a process of discovery.

Try: What's blocking me is . . .

NOW WITH SPIRITUAL LEARNING

Now we will explore unconscious spiritual learning. We can use sentence stems for this as well:

- God is . . .
- The most important thing I learned about God is . . .
- If I'm in the presence of God, I must . . .
- If I change a religious belief, the result will be . . .
- What I never question spiritually is . . .

Be playful with this. I know such learning is "serious," but insights cannot be forced. Once you have an insight about your hidden learning, whether spiritual or not, reflect on how valid it is for you now. This introduces the challenge of testing our early learning, which is the focus of the next chapter, but first some other exercises to try.

When I did the sentence stem "God is . . .," my answer was "over there"; that is, not "here." Again, this reflects some distance in my relationship with God (of course, one of my making). I hold this in tension with my certainty that God is somewhere. Hence, what I never question spiritually is the existence of God.

A PARADIGM?

This is my suggestion for a model to understand early spiritual experience. It includes four steps: primary experience,[2] dimensions, interpretation and belief statements. While this book has been written from a Christian perspective, I hope this model will be able to incorporate other religious perspectives.

We have explored the primary experience of infants and young children. That experience enters awareness through the five senses. It is conscious, but preverbal, and hence not initially available to be expressed in words. But there is an experience that initiates a learning process.

William James explored the diversity of religious experience in his classic *The Varieties of Religious Experience*.[3] Such mystical experiences have a quality.[4] It is difficult to find words, but how might we capture a sense of color, texture, or depth? Like poetry, words can only point to an experience. Maybe a dimensional approach would be helpful:

- personal or impersonal[5]
- one or many[6]
- immanent or transcendent[7]
- eternal or transitory[8]
- clarity or confusion
- unity or fragmentation
- ecstatic or distressing
- life-giving or life-draining
- fullness or loss of self
- sacred or profane.

There can be various responses, including surrender or resistance. It is important to acknowledge that such experiences can be threatening and potentially distressing or even destructive.[9] There is no guarantee that religious experiences are benign:

> *Petra* was born with a club foot. When she was five years old, her parents took her to a faith healing service. The evangelist spoke in a harsh way, rebuking the "demons" that had twisted her foot. She found the experience overwhelming and very frightening.

The next developmental step is interpretation. For example:

> *Kirsty* grew up in a Christian home, attending Roman Catholic mass at least weekly. This form of worship was familiar, with a sense of awe, reverence for the priest and being surrounded by symbols. She could not remember her baptism as a baby, but she always felt welcomed in the church family. Kirsty experienced God as personal, and as plural because she had a sense of Jesus, Mary, and various saints, "but God the Father feels remote." There was a sense of the eternal breaking in and profound unity in the peace. The holiness of Mary and the saints she interpreted as: "I have to be a good girl."

Abdul is a devout Muslim. He, too, was raised in a religious home in which the local imam was often a guest for meals. Abdul "dwelt" in his faith, which was woven into his sense of ethnicity and culture. His experience of God was somewhat personal: definitely one, sacred but distant, unifying and sublime. He experienced following the commandments as "enlivening." Abdul never thought to question any aspect of his faith: "I just believe."

Zeeta is a Buddhist. Her parents were hippies and converted when Zeeta was six years old. The various rituals were natural to her, and as she became an adult she did her own practices. Her experience of the divine as impersonal: "unsure of one or many," eternal, sublime, sacred, and "both immanent and transcendent: both belong to the one rich experience."

Katie was raised in the Unitarian Church. She was taught from an early age to question any dogmatic assertion. In adolescence, "I had a vague sense of the spiritual. But when I got to university I thought that any sense of God or mystery is a projection. Most people *need* to believe, but I don't."

Interpretation can result in propositions. Kirsty accepted her catechism "and I say the creed believing every word." Abdul believed that "I must submit to the will of Allah." Zeeta acknowledged that "I believe in reincarnation." Katie concluded that "For me, there is no God."

This suggests a process of discovery of early spiritual learning. This will lead to the need for testing our interpretation and propositions. We will get to that in the following chapter.

Note: Even as adults, we do not always put what we experience into words. It is left unsaid until we have an opportunity to think about something or talk with a friend. This, too, can be likened to a process of discovery.

WEEK 7 STUDY GROUP

Pastor Mike began the night by asking about people's experiences of Winnicott's transitional object: "Did you or your children have a special object?" Stan and Cindy said that their children all formed an attachment to either a soft toy or a blanket. Sally said, "I still have 'Tiger.'" She laughed: "I'm still attached. He's in my room at college."

Mike explained that such objects provide an early "intermediate zone" for imagining and possibly have a place in forming an image of God. There was some discussion about which sense was more involved. Some people thought sight or touch or smell. Mary laughed: "Maybe taste. My mother complained when I put my 'blankie' in my mouth!"

There followed a discussion about how the attachment object might represent God to the young child. Mike asked:

> If you had an object, what kind of God does it suggest? What is it about God that comforts you? Nurtures you? How believable is this in light of your early attachment. Compare and contrast your present image of God with what might be suggested in your attachment object.

Monica suggested:

> I had a soft-toy elephant. It was certainly soft and representing something big. Is that the idea? I see God as loving. I suppose "soft" and available in that sense. I'm not sure about ideas of punishment in hell. I now look at the heavens, and God's creation is so much bigger than my toy elephant, but to a child . . . I suppose I was headed in the right direction.

Pastor Mike then introduced the idea of hidden learning and then discovery through a sentence completion. He said:

> I tried this myself. I used the stem: "The most important thing I learnt as a child was . . ." I finished that with "I *must* be good." I know it makes sense for a child to want his or her parents' approval, but now I wonder how much I was programmed.

The group experimented with their own sentence completions. Stan offered, "I was quite athletic as a child. I must win at all costs. That was what I decided as a child. I've kept up that attitude and it has hurt many of my closest relationships."

Sally said, "I learned that life is confusing. I think I had to rely on adults to make sense of things, but they haven't always been trustworthy."

And Len said, "My family was chaotic—with alcohol and violence. I was surprised by my response: "It isn't safe to be seen." Sadly, this made sense in my family."

Mike explained that hidden learning also applies to God and can be explored with a sentence completion as well: "Try 'God is . . .'" Sally said, "God is close." Cindy said, "Mine was the opposite: "God is distant." But that describes my spiritual experience as well. Oh, also my attachment style was avoidant!" Len was shocked with his response: "God is explosive. But that describes my father, not my God. I have some thinking to do!"

Some felt stuck in the sentence completion exercise. Mike said, "You might try another exercise. Break into pairs. One says, 'Tell me one thing about God.' There's an answer, and the first person says 'Thank you' and then continues in the same way for three minutes, doing the same thing. This exercise helped Mary to articulate "God has turned away from me." She said, "I actually know this isn't true, but part of me seems to believe it. I think it points to an area of potential growth." Mike agreed and offered to help her.

Mike concluded:

> Well, I can see that these exercises have stirred things up. I suggest that you do some journal work this week. Try to write about how all this sits with you. Allow some spaces and be curious. We can discuss more next week.

SUMMARY

We usually express what we know in words, but that is not always a straightforward process. Early learning tends to be preverbal, and some experiences, even as adults, are not thought about or expressed in language. However, we can identify a transition into language. In this chapter, we have looked at the challenge to backtrack and use various techniques, such as sentence completion, to regain early learning. This can also be applied to discovering unconscious spiritual learning about God and identifying early spiritual choices.

NOTES

1. Bruce Ecker and Laurel Hulley, *Depth oriented brief therapy: How to be brief when you were trained to be deep and vice versa*, Jossey-Bass Publishers, San Francisco, 1996, 127–201.

2. Martin Heidegger (1889–1976) was a great philosopher who investigated the idea of being and how it is "received" through the senses; see *Being and time*, trans. John Macquarrie and Edward Robinson, foreword by Taylor Carman, HarperPerennial, New York, 2008.

3. William James, *The varieties of religious experience: A study in human nature*, edited and introduction by Martin E. Marty, Penguin, New York, 1982.

4. From a Jewish and neurological perspective, mystical experience changes consciousness; Ralph D. Mecklenburger, *Our religious brains: What cognitive science reveals about belief, morality, community and our relationship with God*, Jewish Lights, Woodstock, Vermont, 2012.

5. Martin Buber expressed the personal experience of God in his *I and thou*, trans. Walter Kaufmann, Touchstone, New York, 1970. Perhaps in contrast, Paul Tillich's "divine ground of being" is impersonal; *Systematic theology: Volume 3, Life and the spirit*, James Nisbet and Co., Digswell Place, Welwyn, Hertfordshire, U.K., 1964, 301.

6. The one may be personal, as in monotheism, or impersonal, as in pantheism.

7. Transcendence and the sacred are conveyed by Rudolf Otto's term '*mysterium tremendum*' in *The idea of the holy: An inquiry into the non-rational factor in the*

idea of the divine and its relation to the rational, 2nd edition, trans. John W. Harvey, Oxford University Press, London, 1950.

8. This might incorporate a timeless or temporal experience.

9. In a 1987 survey in England, 12 percent of people reported an experience of an evil presence; David Fontana, *Psychology, religion and spirituality*, BPS Blackwell, Malden, Massachusetts, 2003, 109.

Chapter Twelve

Evaluation

Now we pause. Reassess. Can I assume that you have engaged in some of the exercises and may have become more aware of your early spiritual learning? Maybe you have welcomed this new understanding. Alternatively, the realization of what you have long accepted as a spiritual truth might alarm you. Early learning can be true or false, adaptive or dysfunctional, and healthy or destructive for your spiritual well-being. There are no guarantees that such foundational messages, no matter how authoritative, are right for you today. Therefore, it is necessary to test spiritual learning once it becomes conscious.

THE NEED TO TEST

First, a natural question: "Why not simply accept what we 'know'?" One difficulty is the early origins of hidden learning. The process begins with birth or before, prior to any cognitive capacity for evaluation. Everything is accepted. It is natural to believe parents and authority figures, but that can result in ill-informed assumptions about "the way things are," about life, and ultimately about God.

In my book *The Storied Self*, I wrote about testing the stories that make up our identities. The same criteria can be applied to early beliefs.[1] It is not wise to uncritically accept hidden learning at face value.

Therefore, this legacy will need to be evaluated. First, use reason. Our society values critical thinking, and we are taught to evaluate truth claims in philosophy, to understand mathematical principles in engineering and to test hypotheses through empirical experiments. Rightly, we respect rigorous thinking. Truth is too important to be sloppy in our approach to it. This is the most natural place to begin a process of testing.

We can begin with the "truths" accepted in our families of origin:

I remember my parents speaking negatively about "colored people." Such racist attitudes were part of my childhood. My father was a captain in the army, and he would tell stories of his company of "negro soldiers." Later, my mother did not accept a daughter-in-law from an Asian country. This was an aspect of my hidden learning that I have since re-evaluated from an adult perspective.

Hidden learning can influence our psychological well-being. Consider the following example:

Andrew had recently retired and now had time to think back on his life. He uncovered hidden learning from sexual abuse. He said, "Uncle Bob would never have touched me if I was a normal kid. So, it must have been *me*. My older brother was not abused." This hidden belief eroded his self-esteem. He had a fundamental belief that he was defective. It was now possible to evaluate his hidden learning, which he discovered through a pastoral relationship. He identified the following assertions—a mixture of fact and fiction:

- Andrew was sexually abused by his uncle (fact).
- His uncle would not have chosen him if he was normal (unlikely: there are many other possible reasons for the abuse).
- The abuse was Andrew's fault (fiction).
- Andrew's older brother was not abused by the uncle (probable fact, which might need to be checked).

Such emotional logic, leading to a sense of being defective, is often evidence of hidden learning. I am not saying that it should be dismissed in a simplistic way as "irrational," but such conclusions need to be carefully assessed. Notice that when we discover the hidden message there is often an emotional quality or a strange logic to it.

Unconscious learning is often a statement about reality. Consequently, it should be tested like any other truth claim. There are relevant skills from philosophy, including recognizing premises and conclusions; using premises that are valid; a clear and precise line of argument; building on substance, not tone; and consistency in terms. Those are the elements of a more persuasive line of argument.[2] While unconscious learning rarely has the appearance of watertight logic, it can help to initially ask, "Is this statement reasonable?" Then put the blowtorch of reason to the logic of the statement. While this is a good start, it is not always sufficient. Other tests are necessary.

The testing process can be more widely applied. For example, early learning can be compared with life experience:

Natalie always felt that she was special. That was the message from her parents when she showed some musical talent. Family piano concerts were staged, and she was applauded by adults who were present. However, she did not go on to an eventual career in music. She lacked the discipline to prepare for a conservatory program. Talent took her only so far. But her belief in being special persisted and contributed to a series of broken relationships.

Natalie was unable to articulate her childhood learning. She lived with a fundamental belief that she was superior to "normal" people. This led to disappointments, difficulties in forming friendships, and repeated failures in intimate relationships. This learning failed the life test.

It is not always easy to put hidden learning into a sentence. Instead of being specific, learning can be amorphous. A good example is low self-esteem. Usually, there is no rational basis for such a belief. Everyone is flawed, but surely not worthless! The problem is the continuing influence of dysfunctional unconscious learning, which can easily become a dominant influence on a life story. Sadly, it can also exclude the positive, which potentially might give a better balance and even help someone to feel better.

The relational test has a role to play. Once hidden learning has been discovered, we might ask whether holding such a belief will affect our relationships. Believing that, what are the relational implications? I have admitted the racism of my family of origin. I grew up assuming that ethnicity contributed to or detracted from the "value" of a person. Of course, this is easily rejected on rational grounds, and many theological criteria are also relevant, but it can also be dismissed on relational grounds, which imply that others will be treated badly. Such beliefs lead some people to join white supremacist groups and even to justify violent acts.

Also consider including the relationship to self in the relational test: "If I believe this, is it good for my self-care?" There is a common unconscious learning among people who have achieved a lot: "Success is worth any cost to me or my family." The job, or in Christian circles the ministry, is more important than health, well-being, spouse, family, and emotional overload or stress. This has been a strong influence in my life story, for both good and bad. I think it relates to my need to be noticed. I fear being invisible and need to counteract that by my titles, professional qualifications, position, and achievements. But at what cost?

The idea of a Sabbath rest is part of God's creation mandate (Genesis 2:1–3). Why did God rest after the six days of creation? You might not take this literally, but we have the divine example of needing a day of rest. It is a commandment accepted by the Israelites and Orthodox Jews to this day:

Robert developed a construction business. He won many government contracts and prospered. In his 60s, he had a stroke that left him with a permanent disability. He thought about the script of his life: "My mother was a partner in a leading legal firm. I missed her through much of my childhood when she was always working. I know something of the cost of her success in family, and later paid it myself."

It was important for Robert to assess his hidden learning about success in business. It had shaped and eventually threatened his life. There was a cost in self-care.

We have looked at a number of ways to test early learning. It is important to first discover it, hear the message, and then test it. Until that happens, hidden learning will have an ongoing influence that is all the more powerful because it is unacknowledged. Then, once it is expressed in words, there can be a conscious process of evaluation based on rational thought, life experience, and relational implications, including the relationship with oneself.

Reflect: Can you write a one-page life story for yourself? I challenged myself to do this. This is my paragraph, written on October 17, 2017:

> The *true* story of my life is that people matter. I would include God as one of the persons important to me. At times, I have lost sight of what matters and even distorted it, but mostly I have found my way back to a life path on which I am comfortable. Mostly I get back there through a sense of responsibility both to self and others. Another "fact" of my life is that I have an overwhelming sense of being fortunate. I do not see any grounds for deserving this favor, which I ultimately ascribe to God. I live with a sense of grace.

Perhaps you can include some aspects of your early learning and how it has shaped your life story.

TESTING SPIRITUAL LEARNING

Now the waters become muddy. There is a wide range of religious beliefs: New Age, Wiccan, neo-paganism, spiritualism and various traditional religions—just to list a few. There are also people who identify as agnostics or as committed atheists. Skepticism comes easily. Such an attitude is common among my friends and, sadly, among many thinking people. Why would we need a sledgehammer for either belief or unbelief? I like to think that a thoughtful balance is possible.

The testing process can be a self-guided one. Yes, there is a role for pastors to teach congregations under their care, but in some pastoral care situations it would be considered unethical if a view were to be imposed with even a hint of religious authority.

We begin with an understanding of unconscious spiritual learning.

The first question is: How do I *know* what I *believe*? This might not be as simple as it appears. Spiritual assumptions are not always obvious:

> There were few overt religious messages in my childhood. There was some acknowledgment of a benevolent but distant God. Perhaps God existed, but this divine being was not important in the affairs of life. My father's family had been Unitarians in Boston for nearly three centuries. A number of my ancestors were active in the local church. The tradition on my mother's side was Presbyterian: liberal, intellectual, traditional, somewhat austere. Having a faith was accepted but no one thought that it should be taken seriously. My parents occasionally attended religious services (when convenient), but I cannot recall any discussions about God. All that changed when I had a conversion experience at the age of twenty-one. Suddenly, the Christian faith was central to my life. And that affected my immediate family. While aspects of my faith have changed over the years, my Christian commitment has remained.
>
> I needed, though, to leave behind some initial assumptions. My conversion brought many fundamentalist beliefs and attitudes—basically, a smug sense of superiority about knowing God's "whole truth." Now I recall this feeling with an "Ouch!", but mercifully it was passing and perhaps not sustainable, given my liberal family tradition. This provided a helpful counterpoint to my new conservative beliefs, and I hope that, over the years, I have arrived at a more balanced Christian faith.

The first priority is to recognize how one's life story has been shaped by spiritual learning, then to evaluate such assumptions, and, finally, if the learning is dysfunctional, to reconsider one's commitment to certain beliefs, attitudes, or practices.

Earlier, I proposed a range of tests for hidden learning. The same tests can be applied to hidden spiritual learning. Is it rational? We might note any logical inconsistencies, the presence of emotional reasoning, the test of life experience, dealing with a "felt sense," and seeing the relational implications.

Early beliefs influence the later course of a life:

> *Mel* was raised in a proudly humanist family. Her parents objected to any form of religious "indoctrination" in public schools. When Mel attended university, some of her friends were committed Christians. She began to wonder about what she had always assumed.

But this applies both ways. It is common for children raised by Christian parents to later doubt their faith and become agnostics or atheists. This also is a process of testing what is assumed or actively believed by parents and family. The question is: "What's true for me?" This is a journey that can lead to many destinations.

I suspect that the test of reason is valuable but limited.³ While it is often seen as normal in our culture, it can result in a loss of any sense of transcendence that may have been present in early life. Critical thinking might even function as a paint stripper to remove the color from such experiences, so I see a value in recovering our first awareness of God.

How might we respond to the supermarket of views about religious truth? How do we evaluate a religious claim? Is it a matter of authority? For example, will a Roman Catholic place great importance on papal decrees? Or the Bible? Or a theological tradition? Or empirical evidence and scientific principles? Or maybe a combination?

We have no universally accepted way to determine what might be true, especially in relation to intangible realities such as moral and ethical principles, meaning, and claims about God.

Theologian Mark McIntosh makes some suggestions.⁴ While his approach is sophisticated, it will appeal only to Christian believers. He asked how we discern the truth—"the basic Christian idea, shared with many other religions, that God is truth, and thus that there is a deep connection between how people come to know truth and how people come to be related to God."⁵ His approach is not detached. He outlined a need for contemplative grounding in the life of the church. The discerning dimension unfolds through the following steps (though they overlap and cycle).

1. *Discernment as grounded in a loving trust in God.* The discerning subject is important (Romans 12:2). Unless the discerning life is constantly nourished by the life of God, no growth in perception can occur.⁶
2. *Discernment as distinguishing between good and evil impulses.* Discernment is grounded in God's own desire. We become aware of lesser desires that capture and distort our perception.
3. *Discernment as discretion and practical wisdom.* spiritual discernment needs an authentic yearning for wisdom, not simply enough life experience (Proverbs 8:12, 17).
4. *Discernment as seeking the truth of God's will.* This attains a judgment of the truth in all things because it seeks God's will in all things.
5. *Discernment as the contemplation of wisdom.* An eschatological vision breaks into this world. This is discernment "as a contemplative wisdom, born in the paschal mystery, touched by the perfect self-sharing of the divine communion, and able to reconceive the world in ways that hold it open to the limitless life for which it was created."⁷ We cannot allow wisdom to shrink to the merely technical, procedural, or self-interested pursuit of knowledge.⁸

There is a deep structure or truth of all things. This is intelligible and knowable. Even a partial discovery is joyful, and the more we participate in the Holy Spirit, the more we will come to know and love the truth of all things, as God does.[9]

But such thinking does not provide the last word on what is true. We live in a postmodern world. There is a diversity of religious belief. My perspective is from a traditional understanding of Christianity. Some other beliefs seem fanciful to me. However, my beliefs would be fairy tales to agnostics, perhaps to some progressive Christians, and certainly to people of other faiths. There is no universally accepted basis for evaluating a religious belief: not reason, not revelation, not tradition, not culture. Some people, regardless of age, will realize this. We cannot be simplistic about the evidence for any religious view.

I suggest a criterion that may add something to the task of testing religious beliefs. I accept that it is impossible to ultimately determine whether a religious belief is right or wrong. Knowing is elusive. However, almost every week the world is shocked by another suicide bombing. Usually, the perpetrator has been radicalized. But can I presume to say that his or her beliefs are wrong? After all, many devout Muslims agree with the idea of jihad. Clearly, an act such as a bombing violates any criterion of "live and let live," but is it *wrong*?

One possible alternative to avoid the apparent impossibility of justifying a truth claim can be proposed. Perhaps we can think about whether a belief is psychologically healthy. But even this tentative proposal is controversial. Traditionally, mental health professionals have been reluctant to label any religious belief or practice unhealthy or immature.[10] Brian Zinnbauer, a psychologist, looked at various historical approaches, using a broad distinction of premodern, modern, postmodern and integrative approaches.[11] If this is ever to be meaningful, it must begin with an informed discussion. We can consider "when professed religious and spiritual beliefs and actions [lead to] extreme or harsh differential treatment between members of [the actor's] own religious group and individuals outside of that group."[12] Instances in which adherence to a religious faith appears to have caused harm can be identified in any religion. What is harmful seems not to be the type of religion but how it is implemented, such that person-to-person relatedness is violated. Harmful uses of religion characteristically fail to extend empathy and compassion to others.[13] Clearly, in the extreme instance of a suicide bomber, this conclusion would be warranted, but also in many other cases.

WEEK 8 STUDY GROUP

The study group began with Kylie saying:

> I'm not sure what happened last week. Len returned home completely shaken up. I know he has some baggage from his family, but he was fragile emotionally. He did a lot of writing in his journal, which I think helped. After three or four days, he was more relaxed.

Others agreed that the previous week had been "very intense" (Sally), "a bit of a breakthrough" (Stan) and "puzzling" (Mary). Pastor Mike commented, "We're dealing with real issues. It's never easy. But I believe that insights, no matter how painful, when accepted can be integrated into a growing spiritual self."

Mike explained the need to constantly re-evaluate what we learn about ourselves: "This follows on from last week." Kylie agreed: "Len shared that in his family it wasn't safe to be seen. Later that week, he said to me that this is no longer true. It is safe to be seen by me and the children. We've created a loving family." Mike agreed: "And, given Len's family background, that's an achievement." Kylie said, "Christ in our lives also made it easier."

Others talked about their surprise over what they learned about themselves. Stan said:

> Last week, I discovered my hidden learning: I must win at all costs. I've done well with my career, so I suppose it was helpful in that regard, but I can now see that the cost was too high. My oldest daughter won't speak to me. She resents the time I was away from the family. While that belief drove me through my adult life, it no longer works for me. I don't have to "buy" it any longer.

Sally said:

> I learned that I believed life was confusing. I needed certainty, and that's shaped my recent years. When I first went to college, I looked to the professors to tell me what to believe. Spiritually, I do the same with Pastor Mike. But I'm growing to be an independent adult, so this attitude no longer fits.

The discussion continued. Pastor Mike led the group in the next step:[14]

> Let's now think about our spiritual beliefs. I want you to shut your eyes, relax, and reflect. Can you list in your mind five things you no longer, as an adult, believe to be true? Then five things you now know to be true? I'm happy for you to keep this to yourself, because sometimes we're reluctant to share what

we doubt in a Christian setting. I want to assure you that both believing and not believing are fine with me. We're different people and we have different beliefs and values. What I'm highlighting is the importance of testing our beliefs.

Later, Mary said:

I'm the oldest person here tonight. I've lived long enough to find many of my once-cherished beliefs challenged and now no longer relevant. I hate the label "liberal," but perhaps I'm more free-thinking now. I appreciate the openness of Pastor Mike, but we had a previous pastor who was very literal in his under-standing of the Bible. He believed that people who disagreed with him were going to hell. I found that uncomfortable. He challenged me but possibly not in the way he intended. I became less certain about what he taught. I'm continuing to think about what works for me. It just now occurred to me that maybe my sense that God has turned away from me is connected to the thought that I have more liberal beliefs. Perhaps a conservative part of me has judged my spiritual progress as leaving God behind. Now that I can express this, I know it's absurd. God is more accepting than that part of me.

Mike said, "Amen!" Later, he asked the group members to recall some of their early spiritual learning from the previous week. Cindy said:

My response to the sentence completion was that God is distant. Yes, it fitted with my avoidant attachment style. But this doesn't fit with what I want for my relationship with God. I'm thinking about talking to a friend at church who I know has a close walk with the Lord. Maybe she can help.

Kylie said that Len had been journaling on his realization of "God is explosive":

Len gave me permission to tell you that he now understands his need to keep "away" from God. It was for self-protection, which is clearly wrong because "God is love" (1 John 4:16). He's doing some creative visualization about Jesus welcoming him and embracing him. He said that it's easier to imagine Jesus doing this rather than God the Father, but he'll work on that, too.

Mike added:

I have a suggestion for the week coming. Can you write out a personal creed? This might take the form of the Apostles' Creed ("I believe in . . .") or it can be in any format that you feel comfortable with. If you feel comfortable, you can try it.

Mary said, "I will. I want to put into words what I've come to believe."

SUMMARY

Early learning can be discovered, but it should not be accepted at face value. This leads to a process of testing, which can be done by reason, comparing it to one's life experience, and noticing one's relation to oneself and others. Those same tests can be applied to early spiritual learning. We have also considered the relevance of Mark McIntosh's criteria for religious truth. To this we can add the psychological criterion of whether a belief is healthy.

NOTES

1. Stevens, *The storied self*, 59–82.

2. Anthony Weston, *A rule book for arguments*, 4th edition, Hackett Publishing Co., Indianapolis, Indiana, 2009.

3. There is no contradiction between religious beliefs and analytical thinking; Anthony I. Jack, Jared P. Friedman, Richard E. Boyatzis, and Scott N. Taylor, "Why do you believe in God? Relationships between religious belief, analytic thinking, mentalizing and moral concern," *PLoS One*, 2016, 11(3):1–21.

4. Mark A. McIntosh, *Discernment and truth: The spirituality and theology of knowledge*, The Crossroad Publishing Company, New York, 2004.

5. McIntosh, *Discernment and truth*, 4.

6. McIntosh, *Discernment and truth*, 8.

7. McIntosh, *Discernment and truth*, 21.

8. McIntosh, *Discernment and truth*, 22.

9. McIntosh, *Discernment and truth*, 217.

10. Gordon Allport, *The individual and his religion: A psychological interpretation*, Macmillan, New York, 1950.

11. Brian J. Zinnbauer, "Models of healthy and unhealthy religion and spirituality," in Kenneth I. Pargament, Julie J. Exline, and James J. Jones (eds), *APA handbook of psychology, religion and spirituality*, American Psychological Association, Washington, D.C., 2013, 71–89.

12. Gina M. Magyar-Russell and James L. Griffith, "Addressing unhealthy and potentially harmful expressions of religiousness and spirituality in clinical practice," *Spirituality in Clinical Practice*, 2016, 3(3):160.

13. Magyar-Russell & Griffith, "Addressing unhealthy and potentially harmful expressions of religiousness and spirituality in clinical practice," 160.

14. This exercise was suggested by Cepero, *Journaling as a spiritual practice*, 58.

Chapter Thirteen

Now for Integration

Discovery and testing provide the building blocks but not the building. That must be constructed. Integration, which builds a sense of identity, is needed. Dan McAdams noted that identity integrates the multiple roles and relationships that consitute a life. Usually, this can be expressed in a narrative: "I was . . . but now I'm . . ."[1] We try out different characters to determine who we are and find one that fits.[2] It is to the challenge of integration that we now turn.

INTEGRATION IS INTELLECTUALLY DIFFICULT

Intellectually, integration is not easy. Alistair MacIntyre observed that current philosophies tend to divide everything into bits, atomizing reality for closer inspection. What counts is abstraction.

Raw data is taken from general experience and formatted in universal principles. This leads to the nontemporal coherence that has become foundational to the sciences.[3] The other trend is what might be called the "contraction of attention" to isolated sensations, feelings, and the flash of the moment. The search is for the concrete and irreducible.[4] While integration is against the current of our times, it remains important to move in this direction.

INTEGRATION IS EMOTIONALLY DIFFICULT

Years have been lived with joys and losses. Some of us have had experiences of trauma; most will know the rough edges of life. It is all too common to have experiences but not make connections. Who is willing to go deep and to face the challenge of integration?

How do we encourage a coherent self?

Sally was devastated after the death of her husband. She said, with tears, "He was the center of my life. I can't imagine going on without him. I think I'm in shock."

Sally faced a great loss. She had shared over forty years with her husband, her companion for almost all of her adult life, but now she was left with a sense of emptiness. Such experiences can remain isolated or connected. Sally was challenged to accept her emotional pain in order to make it a part of her.

I am a clinical psychologist. I see patients every week. I will often go to the waiting area of our suite of offices to meet someone for the first time. Inevitably, this person will have problems that they feel are too big to deal with—why else would they make a time to see me? It is as if the person comes with a large chunk of concrete, which they bring into therapy, held in their lap. Together, we chip away at it until it becomes more manageable. In this way, progress is made on traumas, work or family difficulties, distress about health, addictions, and relationship problems. The eventual result, with successful therapy, is that my patient will be able to integrate this into their sense of self.

Consider the progress Sally made:

* *Negative emotional experiences are accepted.* Sally had to accept the death of her husband and acknowledge that the rest of her life would be without him. She needed to talk through some terrible experiences as his health deteriorated, when one medical treatment after another failed.
* *The refusal of old illusions.* Sally was eventually able to accept that her husband was not always the best husband. His perfection was an illusion. He gave his first priority to his work, tended to abuse alcohol, and had a brief affair with her best friend.
* *A new life script guides a fuller way of life.* Sally came to value her new independence and found deep satisfaction in making some new friendships.

There are two important and necessary steps for integration to occur: something must come to mind, and then be accepted and find a place in one's life. Only then is integration possible.

Both self-awareness and self-acceptance are illustrated by the author Irvin Yalom, a psychiatrist, in his memoir. The view from his old age was better than he expected.[5] In one chapter, he recounted having a dream of his mother and asking her, "Momma, how'd I do?" The implication was staggering: "I have been conducting my life with this lamentable woman as my primary audience!"[6] He ended on a positive note. At age eighty-five, Yalom acknowledged that this book was likely to be his last, so he concluded with words from Nietzsche's *Thus spoke zarathustra*: "Was *that* life? Well then, once again!"[7]

ACCEPTANCE

The challenge of integration brings acceptance to center stage in the theater of life. We can accept all aspects of life as meaningful and belonging to who we are. This includes our shadow self, which contains that about which we feel guilty or ashamed. Traditionally, the Christian faith encouraged us to consider ourselves sinners in need of grace. This makes a lot of sense to me. It describes who I see myself to be and, gladly, my experience of God:

> *Robbie* decided to face her dark side. She wrote down ten things that she now regretted. They included an affair soon after she married: "Brendon never found out, but I still feel guilty. I could never tell him; it would destroy him." Then she wrote an account of what took place. She did not share it with anyone but went to a place in nature. She burned the pages and watched the wind take away the floating ashes. She said, "I can't wipe out what I've done, but it isn't everything in my life. I accept both the good and the bad—both are me!"

We can practice acceptance of the shadow self. While it is not easy, it is the way of integration.

Reflect: Think about the degree to which your life story has coherence. There may be a unified theme. Or not. Have you come to accept the contradictions and possibly intense emotions associated with events in your life story?[8]

This links to Erik Erikson's final stage of ego-integration.[9] Potentially, a person will be able to "look back on one's life with feelings of happiness, contentment and fulfilment, as well as a deep sense that one's life has meaning."[10]

INTEGRATING SPIRITUAL LEARNING

Spiritual experiences can become markers on our journey. Janet Hagberg and Robert Guelich described a response to God in six stages: recognition of God, a life of discipleship, a productive life, a journey inward (including "hitting the wall"), a journey outward, and a life of love.[11] It is not a fixed progression because believers can stall or move to and from, in and out of the stages, but this model is a useful description of progress in faith. I found that the expression "hitting the wall" resonated with my experience.[12] It is easy to look back on crises that led to a different understanding of our relationship

with God. It is also helpful that Hagberg and Guelich tell of their difficulties
in incorporating it into a larger story of responding to God:

> *Jacob* began to adapt his view of God: "I had a perfectionistic God. With abso-
> lute demands. It was my duty to perform. But I fell short and felt condemned for
> letting God down." A series of events brought Jacob to this point. He missed out
> on a promotion at work. His mother died suddenly. And his wife left him. Jacob
> admitted that he had let her down. He reflected, "Though I tried, I also failed
> her. And God as well. But now, as I've made progress in accepting myself, I
> can understand more about the grace of God—which is a huge relief and frees
> me to worship God. Everything has changed."

In this example, we see the difficulty of integrating an inadequate understanding of God. But eventual acceptance of unwelcome consequences and
aspects of oneself can bring a healthy integration.

Perhaps we can think of the spiritual journey as being a "good" story. The
following characteristics have been suggested:

- Coherence, in which everything "hangs together."
- Openness to experience.
- Credibility, so not being dishonest or telling a lie.
- Narrative complexity, with interesting contradictions.
- Reconciliation, in which we find solutions to preserve the integrity of the
  self.
- Generative, with a benefit to others.
- Critical awareness.
- Ironic orientation in which an awareness of different views of the story is
  evident.
- Vitality. with a dynamic openness to other interpretations.
- Truth value, in which there is an attempt to bring truth as well.[13]

The Bible is the archetypal "good" story. It includes what theologians have
called the "salvation history" of the Jewish people. The story continues with
Jesus and the early church. Indeed, God has always communicated through
a meta-story.[14]

> Mine is a story of "doing for God." I have never considered myself to be a
> saint or a contemplative or particularly holy. I am aware of my dark side and to
> some degree my failings. I have some regrets, but thankfully not many. I find it
> surprising that I have believed in Christ for over fifty years and not had many
> doubts. My existential struggles have been with life. My faith has gradually

changed and I gently dwell in it. I have struggled with a need to be seen or recognized by others, but even that life theme does not now feel quite as insistent, although it never disappears. My desire to make a difference, which is probably the other side of the same coin, is slightly stronger.

Integration is a challenge for all of us, and, naturally, it is one that never ends.

WEEK 9 STUDY GROUP

Pastor Mike began the group meeting with a question: "If your life were a movie, what would be the genre? A comedy, adventure drama, soap opera, romance, tragedy, or something else?" Len jumped in with, "I think my story began as a survival tale, but now with Kylie it's more a romance!" Everyone smiled. Monica offered, "I would like my life to be a romance, but no luck so far. Maybe a travel documentary. I've moved so often." Sally nodded and said, "For me, young adult fiction put into a movie."

Mike explained that the next task was integration: "All the parts of our lives have to fit together and often this isn't easy."

Mike put a CD in his stereo: "Let's listen to some of Beethoven's third symphony, called *Eroica*, with a quiet beginning and the horns coming in . . . the glorious theme . . . the finale." Later, there was a discussion about what they had heard. Mike said:

Did you notice when a theme repeats, highlighting different instruments. What about discordant notes? Sometimes there are moments of uncertainty, which become clearer as the music progresses. Can you appreciate how everything belongs in this rich and wonderful symphony? Can you see the themes of your life coming together in a similar way?

Cindy responded: "That's one of my favorite symphonies. I always wanted to play it in an orchestra. I can see some parallels in my life—discordant notes that resolve into a greater melody. Wow! Beethoven spoke my language."

Mike then led the group in an exercise: "Make a list of your regrets. Everyone has some." There was some reluctance, but the group had grown in their trust of Mike and the other members. They worked silently for about five minutes. Then Mike suggested:

Can you give a new interpretation—one that is self-compassionate and kind to yourself? This will help it to be accepted and integrated into your life story. The rough edges can be made smooth through acceptance.[15]

Mary was in tears:

> I lost my husband, as you know, last year. I wish I'd told him that I loved him more often. Maybe we could have made more of the time God gave us. It feels overwhelming but, yes, I have regrets.

Mike responded:

> Mary, you're still in grief and the way you feel is normal. We all love imperfectly. Maybe you can try to accept that you loved with the best "human love" you had to offer.

Mary nodded.

Mike stated that there was no expectation that people share their regrets but if anyone wanted to that was fine.

Stan said:

> I made a lot of money in the finance industry. I chased the fast life. I didn't have any spiritual orientation and now I regret not being more generous. Recently, I've been contributing to micro-finance, but I feel it's too little, too late, and I can see that I had more to offer through my life. I'm trying to accept my hidden learning—having to win at all costs—and how it shaped my life in selfish ways.

Cindy contradicted him:

> Stan, I think you're too hard on yourself. You were a good provider and generous to our children. Also, your relatives and friends. I agree that you could have done more, but maybe "human love" is the best we can offer. And, as Mike said, we're flawed.

Mike said, "Cindy is looking at your life with 'kind eyes.' Can you be more self-compassionate? I think it will help you to accept yourself . . . well . . . as you are. It's a challenge for all of us."

After more discussion and mutual support, prescribed a challenging exercise as homework:[16]

> This is called "Life Compass." It might take a few hours. Get a large piece of paper and draw a large circle on it. Now a smaller circle in the center. Divide the larger circle into four quadrants (like an X but leave the center circle blank).
>
> - The south quadrant represents your creativity, imagination, and play. What would you include there?
> - The east quadrant is in the direction of the dawn. What's coming into your life? What's on the horizon? What needs change or transformation?

- The west is for the sunset, so what's ending in your life? What do you need to let go of? What attitudes need to die? Where's deep healing needed?
- The north is your sense of direction. Who has guided you and provided the love that's sustained you?
- What would you place in the center of your life? God? Your values? Or what? Think about how this forms your life compass.

The group was pleased to think about it and to try it, at least in part, in the next week.

SUMMARY

Discovering early spiritual learning leaves us with work to do. How do we respond to that which passes our critical examination? It belongs. But integration does not happen naturally. Intellectually, integration is not easy in a culture that fragments knowledge and encourages abstract principles. Additionally, there is an emotional challenge to integration. Usually, it is hard work. This is a process that brings profound change as we come to terms with unwelcome events and devastating disappointments. Hagberg and Guelich offer a six-stage model of the spiritual journey. We have also considered what characterizes a "good" life story.

NOTES

1. McAdam, "Identity and life story," 188–89.
2. McAdam, "Identity and life story," 190.
3. Alistair MacIntyre, *After virtue*, University of Notre Dame Press, Notre Dame, 1981, 190–209.
4. Crites, "The narrative quality," 309–11.
5. Irvin D. Yalom, *Becoming myself: A psychiatrist's memoir*, Basic Books, New York, 2017, 233.
6. Yalom, *Becoming myself*, 253.
7. Yalom, *Becoming myself*, 342.
8. Karen Burnell, Peter Coleman, and Nigel Hunt, "Achieving narrative coherence following traumatic war experience: The role of social support," in Gary Kenyon, Ernst Bohlmeijer, and William L. Randall (eds), *Storying later life: Issues, investigations and interventions in narrative gerontology*, Oxford University Press, Oxford, 2011, 195–212.
9. Erikson, *Childhood and society*, 268–69.
10. Tromp, "Older adults in search of new stories," 253.

11. Janet O. Hagberg, and Robert A. Guelich, *The critical journey: Stages in the life of faith*, Sheffield Publishing Company, Salem, Wisconsin, 2005.

12. Hagberg & Guelich, *The critical journey,* 114–29.

13. William L. Randall and Elizabeth McKim, *Reading our lives: The poetics of getting old*, Oxford University Press, New York, 2008, 103–12.

14. Timo Eskola, *A narrative theology of the New Testament*, Mohr Siebeck, Tübingen, Germany, 2015, 7–8, 27.

15. There is a self-compassion scale by Kristin Neff, online: htttps://self-compassion .org/test-how-self-compassionate-you-are/.

16. Suggested by Cepero, *Journaling as a spiritual practice*, 92–102.

Chapter Fourteen

Committed Living

The last of the twelve steps of Alcoholics Anonymous reads, in part, "Until and unless you give your life away to others, you do not seem to have it yourself at any deep level." What do we do with breakthroughs in spiritual understanding? I hope that new insights will lead to greater freedom and a desire to help others. Spiritual maturity is never attained by living for oneself—no matter how aware, integrated or fulfilled one might become. Enlightenment can put the ego back in the driving seat. [1] The goal is not a "self-realized" narcissism; it is meaningful action.

A CHALLENGE

The example of Jesus, of course, is one of costly commitment. But how do we understand the gospel He embodied? Perhaps the insight of liberation theology is relevant: we do not understand the gospel until we live it out. This is a hermeneutic of praxis or practice, which leads to a deeper theological understanding. This understanding is enhanced by spiritual practices, meditation, service, and a place where religious discourse is embodied in a way of life. Virtue should lead to action.[2]

> *Gary* retired at age sixty-seven. He had accumulated considerable wealth as a financial planner. He said, "It's my business, so of course I could continue. But I feel now is the time for my daughter to take over. She's well qualified. I feel I'm just standing in her way.
>
> "My wife died five years ago. I want to do something creative. I've always loved photography, so I'll do a course at the local community college. Also, there's an aid organization that I could help by doing their publicity photos. I can

afford to travel and contribute with my creative skills This might also help me to become more aware of international needs so I can be more astute in my giving.

Making a communal contribution has been found to be a marker of successful aging.[3] Tim Clinton and Joshua Straub linked the idea of attachment to God to three stages of security, exploration, and compassionate action.[4]

ON VOCATION

Of the many possibilities in life, which do we choose to express commitment? Spiritual guidance may help. It is best to think about this in terms of our various religious and spiritual traditions. I found benefit in spiritual direction. I sought a director with a hope of deepening my spiritual life. This led me to Sister Lorraine, a wonderful Catholic nun, who helped me to realize that I do not have the temperament for sustained contemplation, being far too active. In one session I explored my use of money. This was helpful for living out my faith commitment. It is best to do what seems natural to oneself, honoring one's spiritual tradition. Some will read the Bible and pray. Others will ask for direction from a pastor or spiritual leader. And some will simply do what seems sensible.

This may lead to a life vocation, although the twists and turns of that path in serving God are often surprising.

Vocation was central to my experience of conversion. Saying "Yes" to God included answering a call to serve in ministry. I was reluctant, to say the least, but it was my first step. Soon I was studying at the Alliance College of Theology in Canberra. I was inspirited by a text in Romans: "How shall they hear without a preacher?" (Romans 10:14). All this happened in my early twenties—over forty years ago. I went on to serve fifteen years in parish ministry, but since then I have had many roles, all of which I saw as serving God in some way. This has not been without roadblocks when I have had to "reinvent" myself: pastor, chaplain, Anglican priest, theological educator, pastoral counselor, clinical and forensic psychologist, author on popular psychology and relationships, academic in clinical psychology, practical theologian in aging, and now research professor. While this might suggest some flexibility, I also include a place for imagination and seeing a different future. Nothing was done alone: I have discussed options with family and friends. Presently, I am an honorary minister-in-association at Wesley Uniting Church in Forrest, a suburb close to Australia's Parliament House.

Only rarely have I had a sense of "guidance." Instead, I have continued with what seemed natural commitments to serve. I had help along the way and carry a profound sense of the grace of God. And, optimistically, I expect the future opening up of new and different possibilities when I retire from full-time academia at the end of 2019.

Richard Holloway wrote a remarkable memoir of his life in ministry.[5] He has been a controversial figure in the church because of his inclusive views, but his life has included boarding at Kelham monastic seminary, missionary service in Africa, serving in slum and later wealthy parishes, and being rector of St. Mary Magdalene Church, Oxford, and then Bishop of Edinburgh. He was always in ministry, although at times, he acknowledges, more from a romantic ideal and tending to overplay the part in bursts of piety. But serve he did.

The question of vocation leads to a question about commitment. Stephen Pickard asked, "Is it . . . possible to make a promise and to keep one's word?" He drew upon philosopher Ricoeur's understanding of identity as continuity of character. Only in this way can a person be counted on and, indeed, accountable. Such constancy is always under threat, so the "true life" has an appropriately modest, rather than rigid, self-commitment. But to relinquish the promissory character of commitment is to risk personhood. Stephen Pickard observed that to live is to promise.[6]

We are formed as Christians in community. Theologian David Ford reflected on eucharistic worship. In the service, we confess, repent, respond to commandments, renew covenant commitments, receive grace, are blessed, and live in community—what Ford called the "eucharistic self."[7]

I keep reflecting on my spiritual story. While I am in my late sixties, I am acutely aware of a desire to make my life continue to count for something. I have enough wealth to retire, but I like to think that God is calling me to the next chapter in my story.

I am reminded that Jesus said, "Everyone to whom much is given, of him much will be required" (Luke 12:48).

When St. Francis (1181–1226) began to follow Christ, he prayed in the derelict church of San Damiano. There he heard the divine call: "Francis, Francis, go and repair my house which you can see is in ruins." Initially, he took this literally and focused on restoring the church where he heard the call. Later, he understood his mission in terms of the whole church. He discovered a more universal ministry. Francis found himself and then a vocation to express who he was becoming.

Reflect: How do you decide what to do for God? How do you see your life making a difference? What about the people you care for?

GENERATIVITY

Erik Erikson saw generativity emerging later in life.[8] Whom do we nurture and influence? The spheres of influence might include biological, parental, technical, and cultural.[9] For example, a pastor can mentor a younger pastor in the skills of ministry. A carpenter can take on an apprentice. A lawyer can guide a junior associate. After carrying out interviews, Dan McAdams concluded that identity becomes more and more concerned with generativity as we mature.[10]

McAdams also identified some characteristics of highly generative adults.[11] In his interviews, he found a commitment story that was characterized by the person:

- enjoying an early family blessing or advantage
- being sensitized to the sufferings of others at an early age
- being guided by a clear and compelling personal ideology that remains stable over time
- transforming bad scenes into good outcomes
- setting goals for the future to benefit society.

We can appreciate that generativity can be seen as community building, with a focus on the next generation:[12]

> I was the convener of a clinical psychology program at Canberra University from 2009 to 2014. It was one of my most satisfying roles. I helped to train more than sixty graduate students and managed to convey my values about effective practice as a psychologist. This fulfilled my desire for generativity.

Being a positive influence on others can take many forms. Have you considered the possibility of *dedicating* your work? I have done this in my books, but why not in other ways? It is a way of saying that an action can be for someone other than oneself.

Latina theologian Neomi de Anda dedicated her presentation at an American Academy of Religion conference to her grandmother, who raised her. The grandmother spent her life cleaning toilets: "I do it so you will not need to." Her granddaughter is now an assistant professor in religion at the University of Dayton.

I was deeply moved by hearing her honoring her grandmother in this way.

Jewish authors Rachel Cowan and Linda Thal have written about the importance of leaving a legacy.[13] This might not be a public legacy—perhaps our lives have been more quietly lived—but every person is unique, and in very particular ways we leave a legacy to those whom we share life with: family, friends, colleagues, neighbors, students, apprentices, and others. We do not have to be at the end of life to think about this act of handing on to others.

The legacy can include physical things, accomplishments, creative works, treasured possessions, assets, and wealth. It can be highly effective if done with the intention of having a positive impact.

I benefited through a trust left by John and Janet Wicking. The trust funded my research position at Charles Sturt University for five years. My opportunity to write this book is the result of their thoughtful generosity. I have just completed their biography—to say thanks.[14]

There is a Jewish tradition dating back to the Middle Ages of leaving what might be called an "ethical will."[15] Often, this is expressed by a parent leaving a letter to children, offering hope, guidance, and wisdom for the years ahead. It can be a video interview or written down. Unlike memoirs, which are written for a larger audience, this letter is to family.

WEEK 10 STUDY GROUP

It was the last night. Pastor Mike said:

> We our study group tonight. I would like to draw things together and talk about the way we might live to benefit others. Maybe you can shut your eyes. Imagine you are at your ninetieth birthday. What will people say as they celebrate your long life? Will it be about your roles in life? How you raised children? Or about your qualities as a person? Or about the place of God in your life?

Len said:

> One of our children is sick, so Kylie had to stay at home. I wish I could live more like you, Mike, serving God and people. But I have a business and responsibilities. I hope at my ninetieth I'll be surrounded by children and grandchildren, hopefully grateful for any opportunities I gave them.

Sally said:

> I feel my whole life is ahead of me. I don't know if I'll get married or have children. But I want to use my education, maybe go to graduate school. I'm thinking about social work. Maybe I could help to make a difference in that way.

Mike then led the group in an exercise:

> This is called "For Me, for Others, for God." Take a large sheet of paper. Divide it up into three columns with the headings *For me*, *For others*, and *For God*.

Then think about the past month. List anything you've done in the three columns. What does this review tell you about how you invest your time? Is there any room for change?[16]

Mary said, "I help my neighbors and I fill in at the church office. It feels like I'm scattered and maybe lack focus. I'll think on how I can best serve." The next exercise was the "Mustard Seed." Mike explained:

Jesus talked about the Kingdom of God as a mustard seed (Matthew 13:31–32). Often, things begin small and grow in our lives. This is the way to bring change. Reflect on your life. What are the seeds you're planting today? Make a list and include anything, no matter how small, that you're doing. What are your dreams? They, too, are seeds.[17]

Stan was very animated in his response: "I did learn some skills in the finance industry. I know a number of people, some at the church as well, who are in a lot of debt. Maybe I could help them with the practical skills of doing a budget and counsel them." Mike said, "That's a terrific idea. There are people in need and you could help." Sally said, "My hope to do social work might be such a seed?" "Yes!" Mike agreed.

At the end of the night, Mike took out a ball of string. He said, "I'll start. This group has meant a lot to me. This is the first group on early spirituality that I've led. I think it's important for ministry and I've made a start with you. Thanks for your curiosity, openness, and trust."

Sally wanted to go next, Mike handed her the ball of string, holding on to an end. She said, "I feel like the group has helped me understand more of myself. I feel more determined to apply myself, to prepare professionally and ultimately to make a difference."

Len took the ball: "I think I've been given another chance. I find myself more accepting of my life, but I want to be wise about what I'll do. I know I can talk to any of you in the future."

Monica was excited: "I've been thinking about how big God is. I think I'd like to do some theological study, maybe with an online course. But, of course, I could move again and study somewhere if there were a good opportunity."

Stan said, "I'm excited by the financial care idea. I know that's something I can do and I think it will help to change that 'succeed at any cost' script that's dominated my life."

Cindy was the last to take the ball of string, She thought for a moment: "I want to use my music. I want to try to compose some worship choruses. I'm not sure that any will be sung, but it will be my offering to God. That's enough."

The lines of string intersected with the members of the group, weaving people together into an interconnected whole.

Pastor Mike suggested:

> My last homework. I encourage you to write out a personal mission statement. I've done that a few times and found it useful. It helps me to be more focused in my commitments. I've also done mission statements in organizations, usually with less sense of any personal benefit. A personal focus is most useful—at least for me. Your statement can be just a phrase or a paragraph. I think it's helpful to do it in an attitude of prayer. Thanks for being a wonderful group.

SUMMARY

Neil Millar has proposed an integrative approach to reflective practice in ministry and professional work. He called this an "ontological" approach. This is not so much philosophical but has a focus on the substance of the person: "What must I *be* to help?"[18]—perhaps "*Who* must I be to help?" It is not sufficient to be technically competent, to be critically reflective, or even to have a capacity for imagination. Introspection and an ability to grow in practical wisdom are equally important. This tells us why self-understanding is so important in ministry. When this is successful, a person does not have to tell us who they are, but simply show us by their actions.[19] The natural implication is *who we become.*

And how do we express it? A life in Christ is always open. Attention shifts from self to others. Life will flow on. This happens when commitment is fired by spiritual imagination. The new story is one for others, clarified by our values, sense of service, and participation in the Christian community. Good things are best shared.

We have considered the role of promises in shaping character and Erikson's idea of generativity. I and others have suggested dedicating one's work, and leaving a legacy and an ethical will.

NOTES

1. Richard Rohr, *Falling upward: A spirituality for the two halves of life*, Jossey-Bass, San Francisco, 2011, 66.

2. Charles Pinches, "The virtues of aging," in Stanley Hauerwas, Carole B. Stoneking, Keith G. Meador, and David Cloutier (eds), *Growing old in Christ*, William B. Eerdmans, Grand Rapids, Michigan, 2003, 202–25.

3. Mary M. Gergen and Kenneth I. Gergen, "Positive aging," in Jaber F. Gubrium and James A. Holstein (eds), *Ways of aging*, Blackwell, Oxford, U.K., 2003, 207–8.

4. Clinton & Straub, *God attachment*, 184.

5. Richard Holloway, *Leaving Alexandria: A memoir of faith and doubt*, Canongate, Edinburgh, 2012.

6. Stephen Pickard, *Theological foundations for collaborative ministry*, Ashgate, Surrey, U.K., 2009, 221.

7. David Ford, *Self and salvation: Being transformed*, Cambridge University Press, Cambridge, 1999, 162.

8. Erikson, *Childhood and society*, 266–68.

9. Robert L. Rubinstein, "The engagement of life history and life review among the aged: A research case study," *Journal of Aging Studies*, 1995, 9(3):187–203.

10. Dan P. McAdams, *The stories we live by: Personal myths and the making of a self*, William Morrow, New York, 1993, 232.

11. Dan P. McAdams, Ann Diamond, Ed de St. Aubin, and Elizabeth Mansfield, "Stories of commitment: The psychosocial construction of generative lives," *Journal of Personality and Social Psychology*, 1997, 72(3):678–94.

12. George E. Vaillant, *Aging well: Surprising guideposts to a happier life from the landmark Harvard Study of Adult Development*, Little, Brown and Co., Boston, Massachusetts, 2002, 113–39.

13. Rachel Cowan and Linda Thal, *Wise aging: Living with joy, resilience and spirit*, Behrman House, Springfield, New Jersey, 2015, 281–303.

14. Bruce A. Stevens, *A lasting shine: The legacy of John and Janet Wicking*, J.O. and J.R. Wicking Trust, managed by Equity Trustees, Melbourne, Victoria, 2019.

15. Cowan and Thal, *Wise aging*, 292–96.

16. Calhoun, *Spiritual disciplines handbook*, 169.

17. Exercise suggested by Cepero, *Journaling as a spiritual practice*, 86.

18. Neil R. Millar, "Up close and professional: Integrative reflection in theory and practice," PhD thesis, University of Canberra (submitted and accepted August 2018), 65.

19. Frits de Lange. "Inventing yourself: How older adults deal with the pressure of later-modern identity construction," in Gary Kenyon, Ernst Bohlmeijer, and William L. Randall (eds), *Storying later life: Issues, investigations and interventions in narrative gerontology*, Oxford University Press, Oxford, 2011, 58.

Chapter Fifteen

Early Spirituality in Ministry

In previous chapters, we have followed the progress of a study group over ten weeks. In this last chapter, we consider other applications of early spiritual learning. The early learning model is practical and can be used in different forms of ministry, such as preaching, ecumenical studies, Christian education, self-care, and spiritual direction.

FATHER NELSON AND PREACHING

Father Nelson is the rector of St. Stephen's, an inner-city Episcopal church. The previous rector was part-time, and the church continued to decline. The bishop of the diocese made it a mission district, so the rector is expected to have a ministry with refugees settling in the area. Nelson was appointed, and after a year or so the congregation grew to a healthy size—although it was still not financially independent.

The congregation has a diversity of religious views, as Nelson explained:

> More than the average parish. There are now people who do not identify as Christian, including Buddhists who have found the spaces for meditation in our services appealing. I think some people come to practice their language skills. So I have to be more inclusive and bring an interfaith perspective. I had to find a way to emphasize a common foundation in spirituality, not religion.

He planned a preaching series on early spirituality. He made the sermons engaging with rich imagery and opportunities to share experiences. A number of people in the congregation had limited experience of Christian worship, so they did not realize that he was doing something unusual. The first sermon he gave was on memories. He explained that one role of the church is to preserve a sacred memory and to tell stories. He asked his congregation to share their first memory in small groups, along with an early spiritual experience. He explained how formative such memories can be for a spiritual perspective on life. Many in his congregation were baptized as infants, and he asked them to consider the significance of the church welcoming them even before they had language or could recall memories. There was a parallel in his church welcoming unbaptized adults into worship and the life of the community. Interestingly, after the service, a couple of the adults asked how they might be prepared for baptism.

The second sermon was on the senses, but it was placed at the end of the service. He carefully prepared the worship service. He asked people to examine the stained-glass windows, see the flowers, smell the incense, taste the sacrament of Holy Communion, and feel the sensation of kneeling before the altar. The sermon followed, and he explained that each person has a preferred sense for experiencing God. He had some suggestions for how they might consciously build on that sense as an established pathway in relating to God.

The third sermon was on the discovery of early learning through sentence completion. Nelson called it "God is . . ." This was somewhat frustrating. Many of the people couldn't get into the exercise, although for a few it was a profound experience. Nelson encouraged the congregation to persist during the week and included a number of sentence stems in the weekly newssheet as a guide. He developed a handout on the dimensions of religious experience and had people use the Early Spirituality Profile grid (see Appendix). Almost everyone joined in this exercise. The results were shared, and many recognized how their religious experiences varied.

The last sermon of the series was called "Seeds of Faith." He asked his congregation to consider how they might serve God in small ways—hence the notion of seeds. He explained: "We begin with our Lord's example of a mustard seed that grows (Matthew 13:31–32). How can we plant such seeds?" He used visualization: "Can you see Jesus standing before you? He gives you a mustard seed. Where will you plant it? What will it become? How can you be faithful to nurture your ministry?" This was followed by a period of silence, and then he asked people to share their "seeds" in small groups.

The sermons stimulated considerable interest among Nelson's congregation. A number asked, "Can we have a regular study group to go deeper into this topic?" Nelson smiled and said, "I think that can be arranged. I was looking for a topic for our Lenten study groups."

ASSISTANT PROFESSOR MARK AND AN ACADEMIC PAPER

Dr. Mark serves on the staff at an ecumenical institute and gives classes at a local seminary. He came across a paper on early spirituality and thought that it might be a way forward for ecumenical and interfaith conversations. He reflected: "There's some common ground. A child can have early experiences before he or she becomes committed to religious beliefs. Can we step back from religious dogma?" He hoped to present his ideas at a national conference. He had his interfaith studies class fill out the Early Spirituality Profile and later he analyzed the results.

Mark started writing the paper. He thought:

> I can see from the matrix that my students had very different experiences of God. Some experiences are more transcendent or just *beyond* the normal. And this is from a seminary class! I can only imagine that the results would be more diverse at a state university. If I can get this paper done, it might be worth a later study.

He discussed some of his ideas with colleagues at the institute. Some contributed to his thinking. One thought that recovering a sense of early experiences might make people more open to the experiences of others, perhaps encouraging curiosity and eventually diversity. Another suggested that those recovering early experiences might become less tightly bound to the literalness of their creeds and be open to the formative experiences of others—even when it led them to different conclusions. Mark thought about the direction of his thinking:

> I previously thought that the idea of spirituality was a bit of a cop-out. A justification for sloppy thinking. Many theologians would agree because we're trained in logic and rational arguments. But now I see that spirituality better captures those first experiences, which can take many shapes. In fact, it can provide a phenomenological ground for spirituality based on early experiences.

He presented his paper at the conference and was encouraged to prepare it for a peer-reviewed journal.

GILLIAN AS DIRECTOR OF CHRISTIAN EDUCATION

Gillian is an ordained Church of Christ minister and is Director of Christian Education at a large suburban church on the outskirts of a major city. She is one of six clergy on the staff of the church. Gillian is also on the editorial board of a publisher of children's Christian education material. She came across some research related to early spirituality and proposed an introductory program to the senior pastor and the eldership committee: "I would like to trial six-week Sunday school classes in early spirituality. I could prepare something for ages 4 to 8." She proposed a pilot program, which, if successful, might provide useful data for her publisher to consider developing further. She was encouraged to go ahead with the project.

Gillian developed and photocopied guidelines for the Sunday school teachers. She made the classes participatory and experiential. She included the following topics.

Week 1: When do you think about God? The teachers asked their classes what led them to think about God. Answers ranged from being in church, to hearing "happy music," to playing in the park. Teachers asked whether the students had had any experiences of God when they were younger. This led to a discussion of memories, with an emphasis on early joyful experiences. The intention was to find a happy foundation for faith, if possible.

Week 2: Draw a picture of God. Some children drew an old man on a throne surrounded by angels, others drew Jesus, and a few pictures were abstract or symbolic with a cross. One young girl, a mystic in the making, drew a dark void. The teachers discussed how we can relate to God through our five senses, but might be different in which sense we prefer. The children were excited to find that they were different but in some ways much the same.

Week 3: Mindful attention to a flower. Teachers brought flowers for their classes to think about. Teachers of the younger students were encouraged to do mindful eating with a raisin and get feedback on how the children experienced the difference between mindful eating and "gobbling." Some classes were able to focus, but not all. The mindfulness of food led to requests for "more raisins please." The flower meditation led to discussion about how God makes everything and how we can be as close to God in nature as in church. The teachers led discussions about what experiences were "special." What did the children remember and what did they forget? Did they remember any special experiences in church or when church people gathered?

Week 4: Visualization of Jesus. The teachers explained that the students were to do something with their imagination. Could they see Jesus in their minds? "Imagine Him with you, so close you could touch Him. What would you say to Him? Feel free to ask Him anything on your mind. Did He say something back?" This led to many different responses. The children were asked to draw a picture of their family members. There was a discussion about relating to parents. How do we get their attention? When do we feel close and when distant? How might we get God's attention?

Week 5: Attachment objects. The children were asked about any object that was special to them as young children. A blanket? A soft toy? The teacher explained how God also soothed and comforted His children. Did the object "say" anything about their relationship with God? The children discussed their favorite thing and why it was important to them now. Is God a "thing" or a "person"?

Week 6: Do something for God. What does God ask of a child? Can we do anything special for God? The teachers were encouraged to use the think–pair–share strategy (reflect, discuss in pairs, and share in class).[1] This led to a variety of answers, from giving money, to writing to the children of missionaries, to helping with a working bee at church. The teachers were encouraged to share why they taught in Sunday school and how this was doing something for God.

Gillian thought that the pilot program was generally successful but that there was plenty of room for improvement, especially by refining developmentally appropriate exercises. She thought there would be value in further research and trials with various age groups. It was promising.

MARGARET AT A PRAYER RETREAT

Margaret served in campus ministry. She had a difficult year. A colleague had to leave the ministry:

> It was a bit of a scandal, actually. I felt embarrassed and had to work hard to cover his commitments until a replacement came. The year was a blur, and I was glad to get away to the retreat center for unstructured time and plenty of silence.

She made a daily appointment to see the director of the center:

> . . . just to keep me on track. I told her about my overwhelming sense of responsibility, how it drove and exhausted me. She suggested that I work on my earliest spiritual experiences, before any sense of obligation developed, to either parents or God.

Margaret did the Early Spirituality Profile and found that she had a personal, loving, and accepting experience of God. That was her spiritual orientation, but now it seemed distant: "There was no sense of judgment, so guilt was foreign to me." Things began to change later in her childhood: "I was the oldest in my family, so naturally I took responsibility to look after my brothers and sister. Later, I mixed that up with what God required of me!"

In the retreat, she started to think about the rhythms of her early family life. She had chores but plenty of time to play. There was a park near her house and she enjoyed a network of friends her age. Then she did an exercise suggested by the director of the center.[2] Margaret wrote her name at the top of an empty page. She looked at it as if for the first time. She saw the combination of letters. She recalled stories about her name, such as that she was named after her maternal grandmother, who died just before she was born. If she had been a boy, she would have been called Allan. She thought about her childhood in relation to her name. She was dedicated as a child, "so I was named before God." She then found it useful to reflect on Isaiah 43:1–4.

On a large sheet of paper, Margaret drew a bird's-eye view map of the area of her childhood house. She included significant places, such as "a tree I used to climb in the park," the local shops, the house of a friend next door, and the school two blocks away. The church was a block or two farther.[3] She found that this brought back many memories.

The next day, she thought about a "memory box" that represented what was important to her in childhood. Many of the things she identified had been lost or left behind in her travels, but she still had her much loved and very worn Paddington Bear. She thought about the bear: "I think God loves me just like I loved that bear. Unconditionally. I know I was special to God. I didn't have to do anything to earn that love. Wow! Where did I start to go wrong?"

The next exercise suggested by the retreat director was "palms up, palms down." She sat comfortably with her hands in her lap. She turned her hands down to drop away all her cares, worries, agendas, and expectations. Then she turned her palms upward to receive God's presence, word, and love.[4] She thought about what new things she would ask from God—hands upraised.

Margaret came to her last days on retreat. She was given another exercise by the director:

> I would ask you to write your future story. This one is to be shaped by your discovery of your first awareness of God. Think about how you might express the love of God in your self-care. Begin with a blank page. Then start: "The story of the rest of my life . . ." This should express what you most desire to happen in the time you have. It isn't a final statement, but more a working draft that can be continually revised and expanded. But you might find it gives you vision and an exciting sense of possibility.

On the last day of her retreat, she wrote out a schedule of self-care. Then she thought about dedicating her work:

> I know my ministry is to God, but I want to make a special dedication of my next twelve months to my paternal grandmother, Frances. She was always so generous in her love to me. Thinking of her will help me to be better in my self-care and to be more sensible in my sense of responsibility.

BRADLEY IN SPIRITUAL DIRECTION

Bradley is an engineer and a devout Roman Catholic. He is in his thirties, with a wife a few years younger and a newborn daughter "who doesn't always let us sleep." He was troubled by thoughts of "sexual grooming and some abuse by a youth worker when I was seventeen. While there was no penetration, there was mutual touching. Grant was not a priest but he was employed by the parish and I looked up to him as a God-like figure."

Bradley made a time to see Sister Therese, a spiritual director and trauma counselor. He said:

> I want to get close to God, but I think something keeps getting in the way. I attend daily mass at the cathedral and I go to confession as often as I can. But I feel distant, as if I'm not really "in tune" with God.

When Sister Therese asked about his background, he told her about the sexual abuse. Bradley was very harsh on himself:

> When I was single, I struggled with my sexuality. I would look at porn and masturbate. I still do it when my wife is uninterested in sex. I think God hates me when I fail to resist these urges. I'm confused. I suppose I'm very "black and white" when it comes to all this. I get laughed at by my brothers and some of my friends when we have drinks at a bar. At least I can relax enough for that!

Sister Therese suggested six sessions of weekly counseling to talk through the sexual abuse. Gradually, the images associated with the abuse became less intrusive. Bradley found that mindfulness exercises and self-compassion helped him. But, at the end of those sessions, he said, "But I still don't feel close to God. Can you help me with that?" Therese suggested that he see her for spiritual direction once a month for the next few months.

Therese had some ideas about why Bradley felt stuck. Perhaps he had lost touch with his early spirituality. His later faith had been contaminated by Grant. He was trying to get over the abuse with scrupulous practices and rigid beliefs, which were not proving helpful. In their first session of spiritual direction, she said:

> I think the experience of abuse with Grant has fixed your spiritual development in the adolescent stage, but this doesn't work with you being an adult. I'm wondering about your first experiences of God, before catechism and confirmation, before doctrines of God and ritual practices such as the Mass. What's your first memory of mystery or God?

Bradley thought for a moment and said.

> I was at the Grand Canyon with my family on a driving holiday and I stood
> at the rim and thought there is something bigger than my dad or anyone. Who
> could that be? I was curious. My parents talked about God and we attended
> mass, but that experience was overwhelming.

Sister Therese gave Bradley some homework to do before the next session:

> Can you start to journal about your earliest memories? Include anything spiritual
> or religious. Start with your Grand Canyon experience and then include any
> sense you had of God. Go back as early as you can remember. Then prayerfully
> reflect on how this contributed to your image of God.

In the next session, Bradley said that he found the journal very useful:

> I began to recall a number of times that I had a sense of God being present.
> I'm very visual—I did some drawing and art classes at college and I enjoy
> stained-glass windows, which might be a good hobby for me. Well, I tried to
> draw or paint a picture of God as I imaged God to be at each age from one to
> ten years old. Ten pictures, which evolved. That was amazing and I brought
> them to show you.

Therese was fascinated by what he had done: "That is amazing. In the first,
it's just a color without shape. Maybe a cloud. There is a development in God
becoming more formal. In the last one, God's on a throne surrounded by angels—or are the figures saints?" Bradley said, "Saints, as in icons."
Therese raised an idea:

> Bradley, we often have an early experience of God and later teaching and even
> doctrine builds on that and can almost "wash out" the earlier experience. Let's
> go back to your first abstract images. What do they convey to you?

He said, "Embracing love that is without limit. Depth. Mystery. Like I read
about in *The Cloud of Unknowing*."[5] Therese asked, "Was the sense of God
being personal? Can you describe the experience?" Bradley said, "Certainly
personal, because I sensed love and the possibility of relationship, nurture,
and acceptance." Therese noted, "That's interesting because your first sense
of God was loving and accepting. But this changed as you attended the Mass
and education classes at school." Bradley agreed, "I had some quite tough
nuns in primary school. There were exceptions, but all I can hear now are the
harsh voices." Sister Therese nodded and said, "The same happened to me
but I still found my vocation."

Therese asked Bradley, "In the next month, could you design a stained-glass window that conveys your earliest understanding of God?" He agreed that he would do it: "I feel inspired to start now, but I'll wait until I get home."

In the next session, Bradley brought out his design for the window. It was abstract, not figurative, and it showed a journey into the cloud that is God. Bradley commented, "I want to enroll in a window-making class and learn how to do the leadwork safely. I'll make it happen." Sister Therese then introduced the sentence completion tool: "I'll give you the start of a sentence and I want you to complete it. For example, I will ask you to complete 'God is . . .'" Bradley answered, "I think I get the idea. The first thing I thought of was God is severe. I could go on with thoughts such as judging and punishing." Therese nodded: "Hardly the image of God to be welcoming. It isn't a picture of God that you would want to be close to, is it?" Bradley saw that: "Yes, I want to run away!" Therese explained:

Sometimes we have a dysfunctional view of God. It comes from unconscious spiritual learning. We assume things about God because they're given to us by religious authority figures. Or family. What did your parents think about God?

Bradley said:

Well, Dad wasn't religious. He'd make snide remarks when Mom took us to Mass. My mother felt you had to do religious things to please God. She even said, "Your father will go to hell as an unbeliever." It scared me then, and even now, because I admire my dad. I can't imagine God sending him to hell. He believed me when I told them about the abuse. Mom didn't. She thought I was imagining it.

Therese gave Bradley another journal exercise to do before the next session:

I want you to list ten things you first believed about God. Then ten things you came to believe. Can you compare them? Put a tick beside any statement you now believe, a question mark if you're unsure and an X beside anything you now reject.

Bradley brought his journal to the next session. He said:

I did the exercise and there are a lot of X's, and a few question marks and ticks. I found that my early spirituality was healthy and I can now affirm it. I can now see that a lot of my later views were dysfunctional.

Therese said, "You're beginning to discover and then test what's true for you now. That's an important process. When you've had an experience of God, which of the five senses were involved?" Bradley thought about the question:

When I was at the Grand Canyon, it was seeing. But I also felt the wind. As I think about it now, my sense of smell is very important to me. When I'm in church, in the worship service, I feel lifted to God through the incense. It's visual with the ritual of the Mass, but smells are important.

Therese asked, "How can we build on your preferred senses for God? It's consistent that you're working on designing and making stained-glass. Maybe you can look at windows in a few churches or an art book?" Bradley said, "I have a few books on religious imagery, including stained-glass." Therese asked, "How can you meet God through your sense of smell?" Bradley thought about that and answered:

I've been doing more mindfulness approaches to contemplation and prayer. I think it's working for me. I can burn a stick of incense when I pray. I'll try that and get back to you next session.

The next session proved to be the last for a while. Bradley wanted to talk about expressing his commitment to God:

I now feel closer to God. Not all the time, but sometimes, and it feels real. None of that severe and judging God. I've got back to a sense of being embraced by love. Grace, I suppose.

I talked to Father Peter. I showed him some of my drawings of windows. He asked me whether I'd make one for St. Monica's, the small mission church in our parish. I was thrilled, and I'll offer to pay for all the materials. It will be a gift of love from me to God. Actually, I'll dedicate it to my parents—both Dad and Mom.

Sister Therese was delighted, and they closed the session with a prayer of thanks.

NOTES

1. Think–Pair–Share PDF file of the Institute for Teaching and Learning Innovation at the University of Queensland, Australia, online: https://itali.uq.edu.au/files/3065/Resources-teaching-methods-thinkpairshare.pdf.

2. This exercise was suggested by Cepero, *Journaling as a spiritual practice*, 44.

3. This exercise was suggested by Cepero, *Journaling as a spiritual practice*, 57.

4. Calhoun, *Spiritual disciplines handbook*, 56.

5. By an anonymous English writer; trans. Carmen A. Butcher, *The cloud of unknowing*, Shambhala, Boston, Massachusetts, 2009.

Conclusion

You have invested your time in reading this book. I hope that you have found it worthwhile. I have argued that first experiences are important. They are the formative influences in the personal and spiritual development of the infant and young child. But this is a silent realm—precognitive and before any capacity for language.

How do we approach this? We found that what is beyond awareness or memory is best described as unconscious. Earlier attempts to understand this were based on Freud and Jung, but that led to a grab bag of processes. Perhaps more important is research on early learning, referred to by different terms, such as "implicit learning," in the research literature. The pathways to early learning are the five senses, which also help us to understand early spiritual formation.

There is a reservoir of early learning that can be rediscovered. Essentially, the process is putting what has been learned into language. I have described and explored various techniques, such as sentence completion, and explained their clear pastoral implications.

Once rediscovered, our early learning may no longer be true to our adult experience. Therefore, it will need to be evaluated. Various tests have been proposed, but the challenge does not end here. What has been rediscovered needs to be accepted and integrated into personal experience. Usually, it can be expressed as a rich and coherent narrative. There is also a need to go further because, as Christians, we express our faith in the service of others. Early spiritual learning has many practical applications, as we have seen in the previous chapter.

I encourage you to see the idea of unconscious spiritual learning as an open door. Enter and go further: "In Christ every one of God's promises is a 'Yes.'" (2 Corinthians 1:20).

Appendix

The Early Spirituality Profile

1. *Think about your experience of God* using the following dimensions, and put an X on each scale in the following table.

(a)	Personal	1 10	Impersonal
(b)	[If personal] Male	1 10	Female
(c)	One	1 10	Many
(d)	Immanent	1 10	Transcendent
(e)	Eternal	1 10	Transitory
(f)	Clarity	1 10	Confusion
(g)	Ecstatic	1 10	Distressing
(h)	Life giving	1 10	Draining
(i)	Fullness	1 10	Loss of self
(j)	Sacred	1 10	Profane

Is the matrix you have done different from your earliest experience(s) of God? If so, use an O on the scales to describe that experience of God. If you compare the two matrices, what conclusions do you come to?

2. *Attachment to God.* How would you describe your attachment to God? (a) *Avoidant* (comfortable with distance); (b) *Secure* (able to be both close and at times to explore new things); (c) *Conflicted* (want to depend on God but often feel let down); (d) *Disorganized* (more chaotic and unpredictable).
3. *Image of God.* Circle any words that feel right to you: righteous judge, holder of moral absolutes, faithful friend, companion, forgiving, source of truth, giver of grace, detached, the absolute authority in life and faith, inclusive, object of wishful thinking, . . .
4. *Five Senses.* Through which of the senses are you most likely to experience God? Sight (e.g., beauty in nature), body or touch (warm feeling in body, hug from someone, etc.), smell (incense or cooking, perfume), hearing (the Bible read or a sermon), or taste (the Eucharist or fellowship meal)? What is your main spiritual pathway? Can you rank order them 1–5?
5. *Sentence Completion.* You might try to complete the following sentences: God is . . . What I learnt about God as a child was . . . Church people are . . . What frightens me most is . . . Where I felt most safe as a child was . . .
6. *Changes.* My relationship with God has changed over the years in the following ways . . . Can you express this in one sentence? Can you write a statement of faith, like a personal creed, to express your beliefs now?
7. *Express Commitment.* Tick any of the following ways to serve God that you would find attractive: helping others, financial support, leading worship, intercessory prayer, contemplative reflection, teaching children, giving counsel, helping with administration, work for social justice, express musical gifts such as singing, serving in ministry, etc. Add anything you can think of that is not on the list . . . (then tick it if it applies to you). Now look back and see what you have not ticked. Ask yourself why.

Reflect on your responses. How would you describe your relationship to God? Can you express this in a paragraph?

Other resources are at www.earlyspirituality.com.

Bibliography

Allison, Gregg R. Towards a theology of human embodiment. *Southern Baptist Journal of Theology*, 2009, 13(2):4–17.

Allport, Gordon. *The individual and his religion: A psychological interpretation.* New York: Macmillan, 1950.

Anonymous. Promoting independence and agency. *Newsletter of the National Quality Standard Professional Learning Program*, 2013, 64:1–4.

Aristotle. *Aristotle's De Anima*, with commentary by Ronald Polansky. Book 3:361–79. Cambridge, U.K.: Cambridge University Press, 2007.

Astley, Jeff. Faith development: An overview. In *Christian perspectives on faith development: A reader,* edited by Jeff Astley and Leslie J. Francis, xvii–xxiv. Leominster, England: Gracewing, 1992.

Augustine. *St. Augustine Confessions.* Translated by R. S. Pine-Coffin. Harmondsworth, Middlesex, U.K.: Penguin Books, 1961.

Auvray, Malika and Charles Spence. The multisensory perception of flavor. *Consciousness and Cognition*, 2008, 17:1016–31.

von Balthasar, Hans Urs. *The von Balthasar reader*, edited by Medard Kehl and Wemer Loser. New York: Crossroad Herder, 1982.

Barthes, Roland. Towards a psychosociology of contemporary food consumption. In *Food and culture: A reader,* edited by Carole Counihan and Penny Van Esterik, 2nd ed., 20–27. New York: Routledge, 2008.

Bednar, Richard L., M. Gawain Wells and Scott R. Peterson. *Self-esteem: Paradoxes and innovations in clinical theory and practice.* Washington, D.C.: American Psychological Association, 1989.

Beebe, Beatrice and Frank M. Lachmann. *Infant research and adult treatment: Co-constructing interactions.* Hillsdale, New Jersey: The Analytic Press, 2002.

Berry, Diane C. How implicit is implicit learning? In *Implicit Cognition,* edited by Geoffrey Underwood, Chapter 5, 203–22. Oxford: Oxford University Press, 1995.

Bollas, Christopher. *The shadow of the object: Psychoanalysis of the unthought known.* London: Free Association Books, 1987.

Bourdieu, Pierre. *Distinction: A social critique of the Judgment of taste*. Translated by Richard Nice. London: Routledge, 1984.

Bower, T. G. R. *The rational infant: Learning in infancy*. New York: W. H. Freeman and Co., 1989.

Boyatzis, Chris J. Spiritual development during childhood and adolescence. In *The Oxford Handbook of Psychology and Spirituality*, edited by Lisa J. Miller, 151–64. New York: Oxford University Press, 2012.

Buber, Martin. *I and thou*. Translated by Walter Kaufmann. New York: Touchstone, 1970.

Burnell, Karen, Peter Coleman, and Nigel Hunt. Achieving narrative coherence following traumatic war experience: The role of social support. In *Storying later life: Issues, investigations and interventions in narrative gerontology*, edited by Gary Kenyon, Ernst Bohlmeijer, and William L. Randall, 195–212. Oxford: Oxford University Press, 2011.

Bushak, Lecia. Mindfulness vs meditation: The difference between these two pathways to well-being and peace of mind. *Medical Daily*, March 10, 2016, online: www.medicaldaily.com/mindfulness-meditation-differences-377346.

Bychkov, Oleg V. Introduction. In *Theological aesthetics after von Balthasar*, edited by Oleg V. Bychkov and James Fodor, xi–xxvii. Aldershot, England: Ashgate, 2008.

Calhoun, Adele A. *Spiritual disciplines handbook: Practices that transform us*, revised edition. Downers Grove, Illinois: IVP, 2015.

Calvin, John. *Calvin's institutes*. MacDill, Florida: MacDonald Publishing Co., no date.

Cao-Lei, Lei, Guillaume Elgbeili, Renaud Massart, David P. Laplante, Moshe Szyf, and Suzanne King. Pregnant women's cognitive appraisal of a natural disaster affects DNA methylation in their children 13 years later: Project Ice Storm. *Translational Psychiatry*, 2015, 5:e515; doi:10.1038/tp.2015.13.

Cepero, Helen. *Journaling as a spiritual practice: Encountering God through attentive writing*. Downers Grove, Illinois: IVP.

Chapman, Gary. *The five love languages: How to express heartfelt commitment to your mate*. Chicago, Illinois: Northfield Publishing, 1995.

Chun, Marvin M., and Yuhong Jiang. Contextual cueing: Implicit learning and memory of visual context guides spatial attention. *Cognitive Psychology*, 1998, 36:28–71.

Clinton, Tim and Joshua Straub. *God attachment: Why you believe, act and feel the way you do about God*. New York: Howard Books, 2010.

Coakley, Sarah. *God, sexuality and the self: An essay 'on the Trinity.'* Cambridge, U.K.: Cambridge University Press, 2013.

———. Introduction: Religion and the body. In *Religion and the Body*, edited by Sarah Coakley, 1–12. Cambridge, U.K.: Cambridge University Press, 1997.

Coe, John H. and Todd H. Hall. *Psychology in the spirit: Contours of a transformational psychology*. Downers Grove, Illinois: IVP Academic, 2010.

Colin, Virginia L. *Human attachment*. New Jersey: McGraw-Hill, 1996.

Conway, Christopher M., and David B. Pisoni. Neurocognitive basis of implicit learning of sequential structure and its relation to language processing. *Annals of the New York Academy of Sciences*, 2008, 1145:113–31.

Conway, Christopher M., David B. Pisoni, Esperanza M. Anaya, Jennifer Karpicke, and Shirley C. Henning. Implicit sequence learning in hearing children and deaf children with cochlear implants. *Research on Spoken Language Processing*, 2008, 29:24–53.

Conway, Martin A. Memory and the self. *Journal of Memory and Language*, 2005, 35(1):594–628.

Cooper, Adam G. *Holy Eros: A liturgical theology of the body.* Kettering, Ohio: Angelicopress, 2014.

Cornell, Ann W. *The power of focusing: A practical guide to emotional self-healing.* Oakland, California: New Harbinger, 1996.

Cowan, Rachel, and Linda Thal. *Wise aging: Living with joy, resilience and spirit.* Springfield, New Jersey: Behrman House, 2015.

Crites, Stephen. The narrative quality of experience. *Journal of the American Academy of Religion*, 1971, 39(3):291–311.

Crittendon, Patricia M. A dynamic-maturational approach to continuity and change in patterns of attachment. In *The organization of attachment relationships: Maturation, culture and context*, edited by Patricia Crittenden and Angelika H. Claussen, 343–57. Cambridge: Cambridge University Press, 2000.

Damasio, Antonio R. *Descartes' error: Emotion, reason and the human brain.* New York: Avon Books, 2005.

Degel, Joachim, Dag Piper, and Egon P. Köster. Implicit learning and implicit memory for odors: The influence of ordor identification and retention time. *Chemical Senses*, 2001, 26(3):267–80.

Delahaye, Elisabeth. *The lady and the unicorn.* Paris: Réunion des musées nationaux, 2007.

Dyrness, William. *Reformed theology and visual culture.* Cambridge, U.K.: Cambridge University Press, 2004.

Ecker, Bruce, and Laurel Hulley. *Depth oriented brief therapy: How to be brief when you were trained to be deep and vice versa.* San Francisco: Jossey-Bass Publishers, 1996.

Ecker, Bruce, Robin Ticic, and Laurel Hulley. *Unlocking the emotional brain: Eliminating symptoms at their roots using memory reconsolidation.* New York: Routledge, 2013.

Erikson, Erik H. *Childhood and society*, 2nd ed. New York: Norton, 1963.

Eskola, Timo. *A narrative theology of the New Testament.* Tübingen, Germany: Mohr Siebeck, 2015.

Foglia, Lucia, and Robert A. Wilson. Embodied cognition. *WIREs Cognitive Science*, 2013, 4:319–25.

Fontana, David. *Psychology, religion and spirituality.* Malden, Massachusetts: BPS Blackwell, 2003.

Ford, Alexandria Blake. *The implications of an evangelical theology of the body* for Christocentric spiritual formation. *Proquest Dissertations*, EdD Thesis, 2018 (10816332), 1–136.

Ford, David. *Self and salvation: Being transformed.* Cambridge: Cambridge University Press, 1999.

Foucault, Michel. *History of madness*, edited by Jean Khalfa and translated by Jonathan Murphy and Jean Khalfa. London: Routledge, 2006.

Fowler, James W. *Stages of faith.* San Francisco: Harper and Row, 1981.

———. *Becoming adult, becoming Christian.* Blackburn, Victoria: Dove, 1984.

Frensch, Peter A., and Dennis Runger. Implicit learning. *Current Directions in Psychological Science*, 2003, 12(1):13–18.

Freud, Sigmund. *The standard edition of the complete psychological works of Sigmund Freud*, vols. 1–24, edited by James Strachey. London: Vintage Press, 2001.

Gane, Roy E. *Cult and character: Purification offerings, Day of Atonement and theodicy.* Winona Lake, Indiana: Eisenbrauns, 2005.

Gavrilyuk, Paul L., and Sarah Coakley (eds). *The spiritual senses: Perceiving God in Western Christianity.* Cambridge, U.K.: Cambridge University Press, 2012.

Gergen, Mary M., and Kenneth I. Gergen. Positive aging. In *Ways of Aging*, edited by Jaber F. Gubrium and James A. Holstein, 203–24. Oxford, U.K.: Blackwell, 2003.

Gerson, Sarah, Meridith Gattis, and Netta Weinstein. Before babies understand words they understand tones of voice. *The Conversation*, August 24, 2017.

Godin, Mark. Touch and trembling: Intimating interdisciplinary bodies. In *Literature and theology: New interdisciplinary spaces*, edited by Heather Walton, 153–65. New York: Routledge, 2016.

Goujon, Annabelle, André Didierjean, and Simon Thorpe. Investigating implicit statistical learning mechanisms through contextual cueing. *Trends in Cognitive Sciences*, 2015, 19(9):524–33.

Granqvist, Pehr, Mario Mikulincer, Vered Gewirtz, and Phillip R. Shaver. Experimental findings on God as an attachment figure: Normative processes and moderating effects of internal working models. *Journal of Personality & Social Psychology*, 2012, 103(5):804–18.

Gunther-Heimbrock, Hans. Images and pictures of God: The development of creative seeing [1]. *International Journal of Children's Spirituality*, 1999, 4(1):51–60.

Hagberg, Janet O., and Robert A. Guelich. *The critical journey: Stages in the life of faith.* Salem, Wisconsin: Sheffield Publishing Company, 2005.

Hartshorn, Kristin, and Carolyn Rovee-Collier. Infant learning and long-term memory at 6 months: A confirming analysis. *Developmental Psychology*, 1997, 30(1):71–85.

Harvey, Susan A. *Scenting salvation: Ancient Christianity and the olfactory imagination.* Berkeley: University of California Press, 2006.

Heidegger, Martin. *Being and time.* Translated by John Macquarrie and Edward Robinson, with foreword by Taylor Carman. New York: HarperPerennial, 2008.

Holloway, Richard. *Leaving Alexandria: A memoir of faith and doubt.* Edinburgh: Canongate, 2012.

Jack, Anthony I., Jared P. Friedman, Richard E. Boyatzis, and Scott N. Taylor. Why do you believe in God? Relationships between religious belief, analytic thinking, mentalizing and moral concern. *PLoS One*, 2016, 11(3):1–21.

Jacobs, Louis. The body in Jewish worship: Three rituals examined. In *Religion and the body*, edited by Sarah Coakley, 71–89. Cambridge, U.K.: Cambridge University Press, 1997.

Jacobson, Heather L. Theology and the body: Sanctification and bodily experiences. *Psychology of Religion and Spirituality*, 2013, 5(1):41–50.

James, William. *The varieties of religious experience: A study in human nature*, edited by Martin E. Marty, New York: Penguin, 1982.

Janacsek, Karolina, Józcef Fiser, and Dezso Nemeth. The best time to acquire new skills: Age-related differences in implicit sequence learning across the human lifespan. *Developmental Science*, 2012, 15(4):496–505.

Jastrzebski, Andrzej K. The neuroscience of spirituality: An attempt at critical analysis. *Pastoral Psychology*, 2018, 67:515–24.

Johnson, Robert A. *Inner work: Using dreams and active imagination for inner work*. New York: Harper and Row, 1986.

Kabat-Zinn, Jon. *Wherever you go, there you are: Mindfulness meditation in everyday life*. New York: Hyperion, 1994.

Kapogiannis, Dimitrios, Aron K. Barbey, Michael Su, Giovanna Zamboni, Frank Krueger, and Jordan Grafman. Cognitive and neural foundations of religious belief. *Proceedings of the National Academy of Sciences of the U.S.A.*, 2009, 106(12):4876–81.

Kihlstrom, John F. The cognitive unconscious. *Science*, 1987, 237(4821):1445–52.

Lan, Conrado Eggers. Body and soul in Plato's anthropology. *Kernos*, 1995, 8:107–12.

de Lange, Frits. Inventing yourself: How older adults deal with the pressure of later-modern identity construction. In *Storying later life: Issues, investigations and interventions in narrative gerontology*, edited by Gary Kenyon, Ernst Bohlmeijer, and William L. Randall, 51–65. Oxford: Oxford University Press, 2011.

Loder, James. *The logic of the spirit: Human development in a theological perspective*. San Francisco: Jossey-Bass, 1998.

Longo, Matthew R., and Patrick Haggard. An implicit body representation underlying human position sense. *Proceedings of the National Academy of Sciences of the U.S.A.*, 2010, 107(26):11727–32.

Louth, Andrew. The body in Western Catholic Christianity. In *Religion and the body*, edited by Sarah Coakley, 111–30. Cambridge, U.K.: Cambridge University Press, 1997.

MacIntyre, Alistair. *After virtue*. Notre Dame, Indiana: University of Notre Dame Press, 1981.

MacKinlay, Elizabeth, and Corrine Trevitt. *Finding meaning in the experience of dementia: The place of spiritual reminiscence work*. London: Jessica Kingsley Publishers, 2012.

———. *Facilitating spiritual reminiscence for people with dementia: A learning guide*. London: Jessica Kingsley Publishers, 2015.

MacLean, Paul D. *The triune brain in evolution.* New York: Plenum Press, 1990.

Magyar-Russell, Gina M., and James L. Griffith. Addressing unhealthy and potentially harmful expressions of religiousness and spirituality in clinical practice. *Spirituality in Clinical Practice*, 2016, 3(3):159–62.

McAdams, Dan P. *The stories we live by: Personal myths and the making of a self.* New York: William Morrow, 1993.

———, Ann Diamond, Ed de St. Aubin, and Elizabeth Mansfield. Stories of commitment: The psychosocial construction of generative lives. *Journal of Personality and Social Psychology*, 1997, 72(3):678–94.

McGinn, Colin. *Prehension: The hand and the emergence of humanity.* Cambridge, Massachusetts: The MIT Press, 2015.

McGoldrick, Monica, and Randy Gerson. *Genograms in family assessment.* New York: W. W. Norton & Co., 1985.

McInroy, Mark J. Karl Rahner and Hans Urs von Balthasar. In *The spiritual senses: Perceiving God in Western Christianity*, edited by Paul L. Gavrilyuk and Sarah Coakley, 257–74. Cambridge, U.K.: Cambridge University Press, 2012.

McIntosh, Mark A. *Discernment and truth: The spirituality and theology of knowledge.* New York: The Crossroad Publishing Company, 2004.

Mecklenburger, Ralph D. *Our religious brains: What cognitive science reveals about belief, morality, community and our relationship with God.* Woodstock, Vermont: Jewish Lights, 2012.

Mendez-Montoya, Angel F. *The theology of food: Eating and the Eucharist.* Malden, Massachusetts: Wiley-Blackwell, 2012.

Millar, Neil R. Up close and professional: Integrative reflection in theory and practice. PhD Thesis, University of Canberra, accepted August 2018.

Miner, Maureen. Back to the basics in attachment to God: Revisiting theory in light of theology. *Journal of Psychology and Theology*, 2007, 35(2):112–22.

Moon, Christine, Robin P. Cooper, and William P. Fifer. Two-day-olds prefer their native language. *Infant Behavior and Development*, 1993, 16:495–500.

Murphy, Nancy. *Bodies and souls, or spirited bodies?* Cambridge, U.K.: Cambridge University Press, 2006.

Nadeau, Jean-Guy. Dichotomy or union of soul and body? The origins of the ambivalence of Christianity to the body. In *The body and religion*, 57–65, edited by Regina Ammicht-Quinn and Elsa Tamez, *Concilium 2*, 2002.

Newton, Claire. *Transactional analysis—Part III (The scripts we follow)*, online: www.clairenewton.co.za/my-articles/transactional-analysis-part-iii-the-scripts-we-follow.html.

Nichols, O.P., and Aidan Nichols. Introduction. In Hans U. von Balthasar, *Mysterium Paschale: The mystery of Easter,* 3–54, translated by Aidan Nichols. San Francisco: Ignatius Press, 1990.

———. *Redeeming beauty: Soundings in sacral aesthetics.* Aldershot, U.K.: Ashgate, 2007.

Northcutt, Kay L. *Kindling desire for God: Preaching as spiritual direction.* Minneapolis, Minnesota: Fortress Press, 2009.

Otto, Rudolf. *The idea of the holy: An inquiry into the non-rational factor in the idea of the divine and its relation to the rational*, 2nd ed., translated by John W. Harvey. London: Oxford University Press, 1950.

Palaver, Wolfgang. *René Girard's mimetic theory*, translated by Gabriel Borrud. East Lansing: Michigan State University Press, 2013.

Parmenter, Bruce R. *Neo-coherence therapy.* Eugene, Oregon: Resource Publications, 2013.

Pattison, George. Is the time right for a theological aesthetics? In *Theological aesthetics after von Balthusar*, edited by Oleg V. Bychkov, and James Fodor, 107–14. U.K.: Routledge, 2008.

Peterson, Carole, Kelly L. Warren, and Megan M. Shor. Infantile amnesia across the years: A 2-year follow-up of children's earliest memories. *Child Development*, 2011, 82(4):1092–105.

Pickard, Stephen. *Theological foundations for collaborative ministry.* Surrey, U.K.: Ashgate, 2009.

Pinches, Charles. The virtues of aging. In *Growing old in Christ*, edited by Stanley Hauerwas, Carole B. Stoneking, Keith G. Meador, and David Cloutier, 202–25. Grand Rapids, Michigan: William B. Eerdmans, 2003.

Polanyi, Michael. *Personal knowledge.* London: Routledge and Kegan Paul, 1958.

———. *The tacit dimension.* London, U.K.: Routledge and Kegan Paul, 1967.

Preston, Jesse L., Ryan S. Ritter, and Justin Hepler. Neuroscience and the soul: Competing explanations for the human experience. *Cognition*, 2013, 127(1):31–7, online: http://dx.doi.org/10.1016/j.cognition.2012.12.003.

Randall, William L., and Elizabeth McKim. *Reading our lives: The poetics of getting old.* New York: Oxford University Press, 2008.

Reber, Arthur S. *Implicit learning and tacit knowledge: An essay on the cognitive unconscious.* New York: Oxford University Press, 1993.

Reiner, Miriam. Sensory cues, visualization and physics learning. *International Journal of Science Education*, 2009, 31(3):343–64.

Ricoeur, Paul. *Fallible man*, revised edition, translated by Charles A. Kelbley. New York: Fordham University Press, 1986.

Rizzuto, Ana-Maria. *The birth of the living God: A psychoanalytic study.* Chicago: The University of Chicago Press, 1979.

Roberts, Michelle Voss. *Tastes of the divine: Hindu and Christian theologies of emotion.* New York: Fordham University Press, 2014.

Rohr, Richard. *Falling upward: A spirituality for the two halves of life.* San Francisco: Jossey-Bass, 2011.

Rothschild, Babette. *The body remembers: The psychophysiology of trauma and trauma treatments.* New York: W. W. Norton and Co., 2000.

Rubinstein, Robert L. The engagement of life history and life review among the aged: A research case study. *Journal of Aging Studies*, 1995, 9(3):187–203.

Ryan, Tom, SM. Our pathway to God: Sight. *Compass*, Summer 2014, 48(4):14–20.

Schacter, Daniel L., and Henry L. Roediger. Implicit memory: History and current status. *Journal of Experimental Psychology: Learning, Memory and Cognition*, 1987, 13(1):501–18.

Schafer, William M. The infant as reflection of soul: The time before there was a self. *Zero to Three*, January 2004, 4–8.

Schore, Allan N. *Affect regulation and the repair of the self.* New York: W. W. Norton, 2003.

Sigurdson, Ola. *Heavenly bodies: Incarnation, the gaze, and embodiment in Christian theology*, translated by Carl Olsen. Grand Rapids, Michigan: William B. Eerdmans, 2016.

Soliman, Tamer M., Kathryn A. Johnson, and Hyunjin Song. 'It's not all in your head': Understanding religion from an embodied cognition perspective. *Perspectives on Psychological Science*, 2015, 10(6):852–64.

Sperry, Len. From teddy bear to God image: Object relations theory and religious development. *Psychologists Interested in Religious Issues Newsletter*, Spring 1989, 14(2):5–8.

Steenwyck, Sherry A. M., David C. Atkins, Jamie D. Bedics, and Bernard E. Whitely Jnr. Images of God as they relate to life satisfaction and hopelessness. *The International Journal for the Psychology of Religion*, 2010, 20:85–96.

Steinhoff-Smith, Roy H. Infancy: Faith before language. In *Human development and faith: Life cycle stages of body, mind and soul,* edited by Felicity B. Kelcourse, 129–46. St. Louis: Chalice, 2004.

Stern, Daniel. *The interpersonal world of the infant.* New York: Basic Books, 1985.

Stevens, Bruce A. *The storied self: A narrative approach to the spiritual care of the aged.* Lanham, Maryland: Fortress Academic, 2018.

———. *A lasting shine: The legacy of John and Janet Wicking.* Melbourne, Victoria: J. O. and J. R. Wicking Trust, managed by Equity Trustees, 2019.

——— and Maureen Minor. *Free to love: Schema therapy for Christians.* New York: Nova Science Publishers, 2017.

Thiessen, Gesa Elsbeth (ed.). *Theological aesthetics: A reader.* Grand Rapids, Michigan: William B. Eerdmans, 2004.

Tillich, Paul. *Systematic theology: Volume 3, Life and the spirit.* Digswell Place, Welwyn, Hertfordshire, U.K.: James Nisbet and Co., 1964.

Toplin, Marion. On the beginnings of the cohesive self: An application of the concept of transmuting internalization to the study of the transitional object and signal anxiety. *The Psychoanalytic Study of the Child*, 1971, 26:316–52.

Tsakiridou, Cornelia A. *Icons in time, persons in eternity: Orthodox theology and the aesthetics of the Christian image.* Farnham, U.K.: Ashgate, 2012.

Turk-Browne, Nicholas B., Justin A. Jungé, and Brian Scholl. The automaticity of visual statistical learning. *Journal of Experimental Psychology*, 2005, 134(4):552–64.

Turner, Bryan S. The body in Western society: Social theory and its perspectives. In *Religion and the body*, edited by Sarah Coakley, 15–41. Cambridge, U.K.: Cambridge University Press, 1997.

Tygrett, Casey. *Becoming curious: A spiritual practice of asking questions.* Downers Grove, Illinois: IVP Books, 2017.

Ulanov, Ann B., and Alvin Dueck. *The living God and our living psyche: What Christians can learn from Carl Jung.* Grand Rapids, Michigan: William B. Eerdmans, 2008.

Vaillant, George E. *Aging well: Surprising guideposts to a happier life from the landmark Harvard Study of Adult Development.* Boston, Massachusetts: Little, Brown and Co., 2002.

Walters, Sally. Algorithms and archetypes: Evolutionary psychology and Carl Jung's theory of the collective unconscious. *Journal of Social and Evolutionary Systems*, 1994, 17(3):287–306.

Ward, Graham. *Christ and culture.* Malden, Massachusetts: Blackwell, 2005.

Waugh, Evelyn. *Brideshead revisited.* London: Penguin, 1951.

Webb, Stephen H. *The divine voice: Christian proclamation and the theology of sound.* Grand Rapids, Michigan: Brazos Press, 2004.

Westen, Drew. The scientific status of unconscious processes: Is Freud really dead? *Journal of the American Psychoanalytic Association*, 1999, 47(4):1061–106.

Weston, Anthony. *A rule book for arguments*, 4th ed. Indianapolis, Indiana: Hackett Publishing Co., 2009.

Wiegerling, Klaus. The superfluous body: Utopias of information and communication technology. In *The Body and Religion*, edited by Regina Ammicht-Quinn and Elsa Tamez, 19–28. London: SCM Press, 2002.

Winnicott, Donald W. *The child, the family, and the outside world.* Harmondsworth, U.K.: Penguin, 1964.

———. Mirror role of the mother and family in child development. In *Playing and Reality*, 149–59. London: Routledge, 2005.

Wynn, Mark R. *Renewing the senses: A study of the philosophy and theology of the spiritual life.* Oxford: Oxford University Press, 2013.

Wu, Li-Fen, and Malcolm Koo. Randomized controlled trial of a six-week spiritual reminiscence intervention on hope, life satisfaction and spiritual well-being in elderly with mild and moderate dementia. *International Journal of Geriatric Psychiatry*, 2016, 31(2):120–27.

Yalom, Irvin D. *Becoming myself: A psychiatrist's memoir.* New York: Basic Books, 2017.

Zinnbauer, Brian J. Models of healthy and unhealthy religion and spirituality. In *APA Handbook of Psychology, Religion and Spirituality*, edited by Kenneth I. Pargament, Julie J. Exline, and James J. Jones, 71–89. Washington, D.C.: American Psychological Association, 2013.

Index

addiction, 3
de Anda, Neomi, 114
archetypes, 7
Aristotle, 33
attachment objects, 76–77, 89, 123
attachment theory, 9–11, 13, 15, 18
Attachment to God Questionnaire, 14
Augustine, 36, 40
Aurelius, Marcus, 25
autobiographical memory, 38
autobiographies, 30

Babette's feast, 69–70, 73
von Balthasar, Hans Urs, 36, 40
Barthes, Roland, 71
Bollas, Christopher, 9
Book of Life website, 25
Bourdieu, Pierre, 8
Bower, Tom, 33–34
Bowlby, John, 9–10
Brideshead revisited, 76

Calhoun, Adele, 62
Calvin, John, 4
caretaking relationships, 17–18
Chapman, Gary, 76
Chun, Marvin, 38
Clarke, Sathianathan, 74

Clinton, Tim, 11
Coakley, Sarah, 35–36, 40, 47
cognition, 34, 52
cognitive behavioral therapy, 9
coherence therapy, 8–9
consciousness, 8, 35, 38
Constantine, 66
conditioning, 7
Cornell, Ann, 53
Cowan, Rachel, 114
Crites, Stephen, 35
Crittendon, Patricia, 10

Damasio, Antonio, 33
Descartes, René, 34, 53
dysfunctional learning, 2, 8, 83–85, 95, 97

Ecker, Bruce, 8, 84
ego, 7
embodied cognition, 34
episodic memory, 38
early learning, 2–3, 11–15, 25–26, 37, 40
early spirituality, 12, 116, 119–128, 131–132
Early Spirituality Profile, 120, 121, 123 131–132
Erikson, Erik, 18, 105, 114, 117

Ford, David, 113
Fowler, James, 19, 21
Freud, Sigmund, 1, 7, 14, 129

Gavrilyuk, Paul, 35
Gendlin, Eugene, 52
genograms, 23–26, 28–30
God Questionnaire, 19
Guelich, Robert, 105–106, 109
Gunther-Heimbrock, Hans, 19

Hagberg, Janet, 105–106, 109
Hartshorn, Kristin, 45
Harvey, Anne, 28
Harvey, Susan, 67
hearing, sense of, 61–64
hidden learning, 26, 85–86, 89, 93–97
Holloway, Richard, 113

icons, 47–48
implicit learning. *See* unconscious
    learning
integration of the self, 111–115

James, William, 87
Jiang, Yuhong, 38
John and Janet Wicking Trust, 115, 147
Jung, Carl, 1, 7–8, 14, 129

Kabat-Zinn, Jon, 52
Kihlstrom, John, 8

Loder, James, 18, 21, 46

MacIntyre, Alistair, 103
MacKinlay, Elizabeth, 27
McAdams, Dan, 103, 114
McIntosh, Mark, 98, 102
meditation, 34, 52, 119, 122
Meissner, William, 79
memory, 8, 28, 38, 53
Millar, Neil, 117
mindfulness, 52, 53, 71–72, 125, 128
Miner, Maureen, 13
Murphy, Nancy, 34

Origen of Alexandria, 35

Pickard, Stephen, 113
Plato, 53
Polanyi, Michael, 8
preverbal learning. *See* unconscious
    learning
protolearning. *See* unconscious
    learning
psychoanalysis, 7, 9–10, 17, 19, 78

Reber, Arthur, 8, 37–38, 40
Ricoeur, Paul, 51, 113
Rizzuto, Ana-Maria, 19, 21, 78, 81
Robinson, William, 75
Rothschild, Babette, 52
Rovee-Collier, Carolyn, 45

Schafer, William, 18
self-esteem, 11–12, 15, 79, 94–95
senses, 33–74
    touch, 51–58
    hearing, 61–64
    smell, 65–67
    taste, 69–74
sentence completion, 84–86, 89–90,
    101, 120, 127, 132
Sigurdson, Ola, 46, 54
smell, sense of, 65–67
Steenwyck, Sherry, 19
Steinhoff-Smith, Roy, 18
Stern, Daniel, 17–18, 20, 79
Straub, Joshua, 11, 112
Study group
    Week 1, 12–14
    Week 2, 19–20
    Week 3, 28–29
    Week 4, 38–40
    Week 5, 56–57
    Week 6, 71–73
    Week 7, 88–90
    Week 8, 100–101
    Week 9, 107–109
    Week 10, 115–117

tacit learning. *See* unconscious
  learning
taste, sense of, 69–74
Thal, Linda, 114
Tolpin, Marion, 77
touch, sense of, 51–58
transactional analysis, 80
transcendence, 27, 46, 58, 67, 98
Trevitt, Corrine, 27

unconscious learning, 1, 4, 7–8, 14–15,
  37–38, 85, 90

Ward, Graham, 54, 71
Winnicott, Donald, 45, 51, 76–78, 81
Wynn, Mark, 34–35, 40

Yalom, Irvin, 104–105

Zinnbauer, Brian, 99

About the Author

Bruce A. Stevens (PhD Boston University, 1987) is the Wicking Professor of Ageing and Practical Theology at Charles Sturt University, Canberra, Australia. He was ordained in the Anglican Church in 1980 and served in parish ministry until 1993. He is an endorsed clinical and forensic psychologist, who has written ten books for publishers such as Random House, Harper Collins, PsychOz Publications, Australian Academic Press, Wiley-Blackwell, and New Harbinger. His latest book is *The Storied Self* (Fortress Academic, 2018) on narrative gerontology. He has four adult children. He is a minister-in-association at Wesley Uniting Church.

The writing of *Before Belief* was supported by the J. O. and J. N. Wicking Trust (grant number 100469).

Printed in Australia
AUHW020914071220
338181AU00001B/1

9 781793 607218